STAND YOUR GROUND

[ONE SIMPLE THING THAT CAN SET YOU APART FROM THE REST]

BY JOEL PENTON

STAND YOUR GROUND
one simple thing that can set you apart from the rest
By Joel Penton

Copyright 2010 Joel Penton

Published by Madison Press
Printed by Lightning Source

Edited by Shannah Hogue

Cover Design by Daron Short
Page Design and Layout by Velin Saramov

Penton, Joel, 2010
[Stand Your Ground: one simple thing that can set you apart from the rest]
Young Adults/Self-Help/Student Leadership

ISBN 978-0-615-40348-9

Manufactured in the United States of America

CONTENTS

For Bethany

INTRODUCTION

Rejected.

I stood at the door of Brandon's house, and my heart sank as his older brother blocked the doorway. I was about to step in, but he moved in front of me, not allowing me to enter.

This wasn't how we did things. It was common for us to walk right into each other's houses, usually unannounced. That's just the way we did it. I mean, we were all friends. No, we were best friends. Inseparable. The finish-each-other's-sentences type of friends. But something was different this night. I had to knock, because this time, the door was locked. And when Brandon's brother unlocked the door, he did not open it casually. He kept his hand on the doorknob and wedged himself between the door and the frame. "The guys aren't here."

I knew it was a lie.

I could see their red VW Bug parked in the driveway. I had just seen them watching TV in the living room as I passed by the front window. I knew what was going on, and he knew that I knew. The look in his eyes told me the real message, and I got it. I wasn't welcome anymore. My closest friends, my only friends, were hanging out like we always had, but this time without me. And they had sent Brandon's older brother to do their dirty work.

I was rejected.

As I walked backed to my car, I noticed that they had closed the blinds so that I could not see inside. I will never forget the confusion and pain I felt when I got into my car. *"Am I mad? Do I cry?"* Millions of thoughts and questions ran through my mind. *"How had it come to this? I guess there had been signs that we were growing apart, but we were best friends. This just doesn't make sense. Do they really resent me this much? Okay, I know I'm not the perfect friend, but nobody is, right? Where am I going to go? These are my only friends. What am I going to do?"*

> I will never forget the confusion and pain I felt when I got into my car.

Life has a funny way of working itself out. The pain I experienced standing at that front door was probably the worst pain I had ever felt. But when it seemed like my life was ending, it was really just beginning. I soon came to realize that I had been rejected not because of the things I had done wrong, but because of the things I had done right. And many of the best moments in my life happened after I was turned away that night.

Walking away from Brandon's house, I never imagined I would achieve some of the things I've achieved. I never thought I would hear thousands of people cheering for me. I never thought I'd be on national TV. I never really expected to do anything extraordinary in my life. I just wanted to do one thing: stand my ground.

You see, like most people, I had made some promises in my life, some commitments to myself and to others. I'm not sure exactly why, but I had a deep, irresistible desire to follow through and keep my commitments. I just wanted to persevere and do what I said I was going to do — no more, no less. Little did I know that by simply standing my ground, success was right around the corner. This truth continues to repeat itself over and over in my life. It holds true in other people's lives as well. I know it can in yours too. You can do something incredibly significant if you just *Stand Your Ground!*

Maybe, like me, you have felt the sting of rejection. Maybe you've felt alone; maybe you've felt abandoned by people around you. Maybe you've wanted to do great things, but have no idea how to get there. I hope my story can help you find the answer, help you discover that one simple thing can set you apart from the rest.

But for you to fully understand, I need tell you how I ended up at that door.

PART ONE
MY COMMITMENT

CHAPTER 1:
MAKING MY COMMITMENT
"Picked Third From Last"

When I was in seventh grade, I made a commitment that would affect the rest of my life. I decided that I was going to be the best football player I could be. Sounds like a typical kid's dream, doesn't it? Every kid dreams of one day winning the Super Bowl...right?

Well, in my case, it wasn't just an average kid's dream. I had no illusions of the Super Bowl, no grand dreams about getting a lot of playing time. What I wanted, more than anything, was just to play ball.

And for me, *that* dream was almost as far away as the Super Bowl.

A ROUGH START

"We Penton men are born with a lot of desire to play sports, but not much ability," my father stated in his matter-of-fact voice, frequently throughout my childhood.

He was totally right. I was bad at sports, and I knew it.

I'm from a small town in northwest Ohio called Van Wert, where there is a lot of corn and not a lot of people. In Van Wert, everyone knows each other. There are only a handful of traffic lights and two decent restaurants, one of which is Pizza Hut.

But I loved it. And like many small towns, sports was an important part of the community. Unfortunately, I was one of the worst athletes in my area. Think I'm exaggerating? Sadly, I'm not. Let me prove it to you.

We often ran races at my elementary school, and I was so slow that I earned the nickname, "Slow Motion Man." And while I had almost no speed, somehow I had even less hand-eye coordination. I discovered this at the age of eight. My best friend Jeff and I often played baseball at the park. After a bit of pitch and catch, we hit each other ground balls. Well, really Jeff just hit balls to me because I could never get the hang of throwing the ball up in the air and hitting it with the bat.

I WAS so slow that I earned the nickname, "Slow Motion Man."

But that didn't bother me too much. I just enjoyed playing.

Things didn't get any better when I was old enough to play organized sports. First I tried a YMCA basketball league. My team was awful. I remember one kid in particular, named Alex, who couldn't get the basketball all the way up to the rim. In our last game of the season, after a running start, he managed to hit the bottom of the backboard. This great accomplishment inspired applause from our parents and laughter from the opposing team. But I didn't contribute much either. I had no confidence in my dribbling abilities, so whenever I got the ball, I just froze. The other team would then converge on me and try to slap the ball out of my hands. Next came the predictable sound of the referee's whistle for a jump ball. The game would also end predictably, with the other team celebrating, and our team going home, defeated, again. Still, somehow I loved it.

As I got older, sports became more competitive, and tryouts became the norm. At tryouts, each kid was pitted against the others to determine who had the skill to compete at the next level. And when I was compared to the other kids, my lack of athletic skill became even more obvious.

My first tryout was for Little League baseball at the age of nine. I was a little bit older than the other guys in my grade. And because Little League divisions were based on age, not grade, I got to try out a full year earlier than my friends. I worked hard that Spring in the weeks leading up to tryouts. Every day, when my dad got home from work, we practiced my throwing and catching in the front yard. On weekends he took me to the batting cage so I could perfect my swing.

As the day of tryouts slowly approached, I remember my dad trying to prepare me mentally as well as physically. "You know, son, in Little League the ages are 9-12, so 9-year-olds rarely get picked to play the first year they try out." He went on to say that I would most likely have to try out a couple of years, maybe even three years in a row, before I would get picked. I guess he realized, even then, that there wasn't much hope of me making a team. And he didn't want me to be too disappointed.

But I didn't care that I might not get picked. I was eager to try out.

During tryouts, I played just as hard as I had practiced every night with my dad. After all the players had taken turns hitting, throwing, and catching, the league administrators explained the selection process. All the players would go home. Then the coaches would confer and select their teams. Each player who was picked for a team would receive a phone call from his new coach sometime within the next few days. If a player wasn't picked, he would not get a phone call. I excitedly returned home and told my dad all about the tryout. I felt confident that my hard work had paid off, so I sat and waited patiently by the phone.

And...the phone rang!

I grabbed it immediately and answered, "Hello?" It was a neighbor asking for my mom. A few hours later it rang again! With a little less anticipation this time, I answered, "Hello?" It was my aunt, this time asking for my dad. The phone continued to ring, and each time I was a little less hopeful and a little more disappointed. For several days I waited for a call that would not come.

Finally, I came to terms with reality: I had not been picked.

So, instead of playing Little League that year, I played in the "Farm League" (aka "Loser League"). We played our games on the girls' softball field, wearing matching t-shirts with the words "Farm League" spelled out in big block letters on the front, clearly proclaiming to everyone who saw us that we had failed to make the Little League teams.

Even worse, the Little League teams played on their own field next to ours, often at the same time. I longingly gazed over the fence at their matching hats and jerseys as they ran onto the field made just for them. Everything about them seemed perfect, right down to their baseball cleats and gleaming white socks and pants. To be honest...I envied them. But, at the same time, I wasn't too concerned. My dad had prepared me for this. "No big deal," I thought, "Next year is MY year."

Finally, after what seemed like an eternity, the next spring came. I was pumped for tryouts, and so were my friends. But since they were just 9-year-olds and it was their first time trying out, I tried to prepare them for the inevitable disappointment. I, on the other hand, was a 10-year-old with a full year of experience under my belt. This year things would surely be different.

Again, I practiced for countless hours with my dad, sometimes late into the evening. At tryouts, I played hard. I eagerly returned home and waited by the phone. This time it rang, and it was for me!

It was my friend Justin, telling me that he had been picked. Phone call after phone call was for me. My friends were all telling me how they had been picked and what team they were now on.

But once again, my phone call from a coach never came.

How did this happen? They were 9; I was 10. It was their first tryout; it was my second. They played in matching hats on the good field; I had to play in the "Farm League" again. I was crushed and embarrassed. But I managed to recover, mostly thanks to my dad's encouragement. I did have fun playing ball, but it was clear that I still had not found my sport.

I started thinking to myself, "Well, maybe I'm not the best at basketball or baseball, but I know there is something out there for me."

And I soon discovered what that was.

PERFECT...WITH A PROBLEM

Without a doubt, football seemed to be the perfect sport for me.

Different positions on the team meant different types of skills. Those who couldn't run fast, jump high, catch, or throw could still play on the line where simple, blunt aggression was encouraged. On the football field, I could concentrate on hitting a much bigger target than a hoop or a player's mitt – I could hit *people*. I remember clearly thinking, "I can do things on the football field that would get me thrown into jail if I did them in everyday life." But on the field, the harder I hit, the more praise I

> On the football field, I could concentrate on hitting a much bigger target than a hoop or a player's mitt — I could hit people.

would get from coaches. It was awesome.

"Now this is the sport for me," I thought.

I tried out for the Van Wert City youth football league, along with about fifty other guys, on a hot August day. We ran through several agility drills and attempted to pass, catch, and kick. I did what they asked and tried to show my enthusiasm as a potential lineman. When the tryout came to an end, the coaches gathered all the players together and had us sit Indian-style in the shade of a large oak tree at the west end of the field.

This time, instead of being sent home to await a phone call, I was surprised to see parents and former players arrive. The four coaches frantically scribbled notes on their clipboards and then stood up in front of us. The returning players gathered behind each coach; many were attempting to sneak a peek at their coach's clipboard. At first, I wasn't sure what exactly was going on, but I quickly figured it out. They were going to start picking teams right then and there...in front of everyone!

I immediately got nervous as I considered what was about to take place. Players picked first would receive recognition for their good performance in front of the crowd. However, players picked last, or not picked at all, would experience not only personal rejection, but also public embarrassment. I quickly glanced around at my competition and tried to make a mental estimate of when I would be chosen. I guessed that the real athletic prospects for quarterback, running back, and receiver would be picked right away. Then, they would start picking the bigger kids for the line positions. Although I wasn't big and strong, I was pretty tall for my age. So I predicted that I would be picked about halfway through the process.

"Michael Stratford," announced the first coach. Ecstatic to be first picked, Mike jumped up and shook hands with his new coach, before continuing his celebration with high fives and cheers from his new teammates. The parents, seated behind us, clapped to show their approval.

One by one players' names were called. After a while, I did a quick count of the group still sitting on the grass, and I realized that the halfway point had come and gone. The sun had started to set. Parents pulled out their jackets, and many of them began folding up their chairs in preparation to leave. I desperately glanced around at the dwindling group. My breathing sped up, and my palms got sweaty.

"What if I'm not picked at all?" I thought to myself.

Finally, with just one kid sitting to my right and one to my left, the tall coach on the far left with a red mustache said in a defeated voice, "I'll take that Penton kid."

Wow...I was picked third from last. But at least I was picked! It was the first time I had been picked at all to play in any organized sport, so rather than being upset, I was actually excited! I jumped up, shook my coach's hand, and eagerly joined my teammates behind him. But they weren't sharing my enthusiasm. The excitement was long gone. As the last two kids' names were called, I realized that *everyone* had to be picked and placed on a team. It was a no-cut league. The last *really were* the worst. I realized that my new teammates were actually saddened that I was on their team, not excited.

And that moment confirmed exactly what I had already known from early in my childhood: I was bad at sports.

THE CHALLENGE

That minor setback didn't stop me, however. Football was soon almost all I thought and talked about. My dad knew my love for the game, and when I reached middle school, he set a challenge in front of me.

He said, "Son, if you love the game so much, you should commit yourself to becoming the best football player you can be." He suggested that I do anything and everything to reach that goal.

I listened to his challenge. I considered what he had suggested and thought about it deeply. "What if I never do anything great on the field? What if it just gets too hard? If I do this, how good could I really be?"

I thought to myself, "I am really going to do it; I am really going to make it count."

I knew there was only one way to find out.

I remember my decisive moment. As I was lying in my bed, thinking about the future, I realized that I didn't want to waste another minute. I rolled out of bed and did as many push-ups and sit-ups as I could before going to sleep. Not only that, I determined that from then on, I would do the same thing every night before going to bed. I wore myself out that first night.

In that moment, lying on my bedroom floor, covered in sweat, I thought to myself, "I am really going to do it; I am really going to make it count. I am not just going to work hard; I am going to do whatever it takes to be the best football player I can possibly be."

I had accepted "The Challenge."

I began to strive toward that goal, and I kept it in the forefront of my mind at all times. I worked hard at practice. I listened to my coaches and gave them 100% every time. I was completely dedicated, even though I almost never saw any playing time at first. Before each practice, I remembered what my father said to me frequently throughout my childhood. But now, with more focus and drive, I was able to remember his quote differently and in its entirety,

"We Penton men are born with a lot of desire to play sports, but not much ability. *You weren't born with great ability, but you can still work hard to be the very best that you can be.*"

And that is exactly what I set out to do. Maybe there wouldn't be a Super Bowl. Maybe I would never start a game. But I had made my decision, and there was no turning back. I was going to be the best football player that I could be.

MAKING IT PERSONAL

1. As a kid, Joel dreamed of playing on a sports team... any team. When you were a kid, did you have any 'big dreams'? Maybe an activity you wanted to do or a job you wanted to have 'when you grew up.' Describe your dream.

   _____

   _____

   _____

2. Now that you're older, are your dreams still the same, or have you found new things to dream about? What are some of your dreams now? Why do you think they've changed?

   _____

   _____

   _____

3. In the story, Joel tried a lot of different sports before finding football. If you were in Joel's shoes, would you have kept at it like he did? Would you have given up and tried something else? Why?

   _____

   _____

   _____

CHAPTER 2:
KEEPING MY COMMITMENT
"Rollin' In My Mom's Buick"

Everybody remembers the first time they fall in love. I was in third grade. For me, though, it wasn't a girl. No, in third grade I fell in love with the game of football.

Clearly, I wasn't the best athlete. But I knew football was just right for me. I mean, where else as a small child do you get to strap on little plastic pads, run as fast as you can, and then slam your body into other small children? There was nothing like it.

So I decided that football was going to be my thing. And it was. Despite my lack of talent, I made a crazy commitment to be the best football player I could be.

But deciding that I loved football and actually following through with my commitment were two totally different things.

MOVING FORWARD

I began training myself physically.

I started lifting weights so that I could get stronger. To figure out what type of workout would be best for me, I read numerous books. I bought a small rubber ball that I carried around with me at school, and I squeezed it constantly to strengthen my forearms. I set up a gym in my basement where I lifted weights and practiced vertical jumping and agility drills. I was a football freak. Although I didn't have a lot of talent, I thought maybe I could be decent if I worked incredibly hard.

I even surrounded myself with people who would help me get closer to my commitment.

My best friend, Jeff, had always been obsessed with football right along with me. We were the "sports guys" at our elementary school, and everyone knew it. When we got to the middle school, Jeff and I met about ten guys from other elementary schools who were really passionate about sports, too. Our group of two was now a group of about twelve. We loved practicing and competing against each other in whatever sport was in season. Our friendship made us all better athletes, and with their help, I moved one step closer to achieving my goal.

And slowly, things began to change. In eighth grade, my hard work started to pay off. Big time.

Until that time, I had been skinny and weak. Now, I was strong and focused. Before, coaches and parents never remembered my name. Now, I was one of the best players on the team, and my name was frequently called out by the announcer during games. I was making plays left and right. I had always been a bit taller than everyone else, but now I was also stronger, much stronger, and it showed.

During my freshman year of high school, my coach encouraged me to try out for the varsity football team. Frankly, I was surprised at his confidence in me. I knew I had improved, but I still thought of myself as an average player with a good work ethic. My coach thought differently. Apparently, he was right. That year I was one of only two freshmen who made the varsity football team.

I pressed on in my quest to become the best football player I could be. When the season was over, I continued lifting weights when all of my teammates took a break. I attended football camps at colleges and studied the videos of my own games at home. I memorized any new drill my coaches had us perform and enhanced it by making it more difficult when I returned home. I spray-painted a grid on the floor of my basement to aid in speed drills. I added more protein to my diet and focused on eating foods that would fuel my body appropriately.

By my junior year of high school, I had improved drastically. I was taller, stronger, and now faster than most of my competition. My success took many people by surprise, including myself. I truly didn't know just how good I had become at

> That year I was one of only two freshmen who made the varsity football team.

this sport I loved so dearly. I just wanted to keep playing because I was having fun hitting people.

ME VS. THEM

Unfortunately, my junior year was also the year I faced the first major obstacle to reaching my goal: my friends.

In our freshman year, the group had split in half. One half wanted to go join the party scene, but the other half wanted to stay focused on sports. And the six of us who stayed focused took a firm stance against partying.

We knew that drinking and partying wouldn't help us reach our goals. After all, we'd seen a lot of athletes at our school fail at their sport whenever they got caught up in the party scene. We were going to be different. We took pride in the fact that we were motivated to do something significant. We were critical of our former friends for choosing to do what they were doing, and we were going to avoid all the negative consequences that came with partying all the time. For two years, this was our mutual understanding; it was our group identity.

But then, something changed.

One night, my friend Brandon went out drinking with some other people. We were shocked when we heard of it the following Monday at school. It didn't make sense. We had decided that partying was not something "we" did, and Brandon was part of the 'We.' Frankly, we were a little bit offended and saddened by the whole thing. It was a touchy subject, so when he ate with us at lunch that Monday, it just seemed easier to avoid the topic completely, so that's what we did. We avoided any discussion or confrontation with Brandon, and after a couple of days, what he had done seemed like it wasn't a big deal anymore.

> It just seemed easier to avoid the topic completely, so that's what we did.

But the next weekend, he took another friend from our group out drinking. This time, we found out about their partying before school on Monday because the remaining four of us wondered where they were on Saturday night. Even though we knew ahead of time, we handled this new development exactly the same way. We just didn't know what else to do. One by one, every guy in my group was pulled into the party scene.

Everyone but me.

I was confused. We had made a commitment. And we had always put our commitment first. I didn't understand how all my friends could have forgotten that so easily. But I knew what I needed to do in order to reach my potential, in football and in life: I needed to keep my commitment. I needed to *stand my ground.*

I just didn't think it would be so difficult. I thought my friends were going to stand their ground with me. I was wrong.

CHOICES

At first, things were mostly normal. The six of us still hung out for a bit on Friday and Saturday nights. Then, we parted ways. They moved to their new hangout place, where they began drinking, and I went home. It wasn't as much fun for me, but at least I got to hang out with them a little bit.

Eventually though, they wanted to start drinking right away, all weekend, every weekend. I tried hanging out with them while they were drinking, but it didn't take long to figure out that this wasn't a great idea. I felt uncomfortable and had to come up with excuses to leave.

Ultimately, I decided that I could not hang out with them while they were partying for three reasons.

First, I didn't want to set myself up for failure. When I was with them, the temptation to drink was in my face all the time. And it would be a lie to say I wasn't tempted to give up my commitment and join them. It was tough to stay strong. So it was smarter to just avoid the temptation in the first place.

Second, I felt like I was encouraging their bad decision. They knew that what they were doing was wrong. But hanging out with them while they were drinking was like telling them, "I'm okay with you doing this, but it's just not for me." And I was not okay with it. I knew it wasn't right, for me or for them. I guess I was hoping that my example would convince them to stop. I wanted them to admit that they had made a mistake so things could go back to the way they were. But it didn't happen that way.

I guess I was hoping that my example would convince them to stop.

Third, even though I wasn't drinking with my friends, being with them was almost just as bad. Perception is important. If my friends got caught, by the police or anyone else, the person who caught us would not be able to tell the difference between who was drinking and who was not. Just my association with them would make me look guilty. I knew that I would be in just as much trouble as them if they got caught. I also knew that this would, again, hurt my chances of reaching my potential on the football field.

Luckily, I was able to avoid a rift with my friends, at least for a short period of time. I was on the wrestling team at school, and it was the end of the season. We had weekend-long tournaments 3 weeks in a row. On those weekends, I didn't have time to hang out with my friends. But this had never been a problem before. If a guy had a new girlfriend or was busy with a particular sport, our group might not see him for a few weeks or so, and then he would start to hang out with us again. That was life. It was no big deal.

What I didn't know was that this time, things were different.

REJECTION

When wrestling was over, I was a little anxious but still excited to hang out with my friends again. I realized some things had changed, but they were still my friends, and I hadn't seen them in a long time.

I took my mom's white Buick and drove to my friend's house.

I rolled down the window of my car and said, "Hey! What's up, guys?" with excitement. My friend Adam took a small step toward me. "Oh, hey, Joel," he said flatly. "We were just getting ready to leave. To go to, uh," he paused and looked around at the other guys, "to Ben's house."

The only car there besides mine was Ben's red VW Bug, and there were six guys. So I said, "Cool, why don't half of you guys come with me?"

"Nah, that's okay, we'll go in here," Adam replied. So I watched, a little confused, as all six of them crammed into the Bug. But it wasn't a big deal, so I didn't give it much thought.

I threw the Buick into reverse so I could follow my friends to Ben's house. Strangely, on the way there, the red Bug started to speed up and take some crazy turns that weren't at all in the direction of Ben's house. Again, I didn't think much of it. When we weren't playing video games or watching movies, sometimes we would just race around town. So, I continued to follow them, determined to win the race, but eventually the red Bug made it through a stoplight that I couldn't run, and they lost me. "No big deal," I thought, "I'll just go to Ben's house and meet them there."

So I drove over to Ben's house and parked my car on the street. No Bug. I figured they had stopped somewhere, so I waited. Finally, after about a half hour, I decided that they must have changed their minds and gone somewhere else. I didn't have a cell phone on me at the time, so I drove around and checked all of our typical places – still no Bug.

Then I thought of one last place where they might be: Brandon's house. I drove over there with anticipation.

Bingo! Red Bug.

This wasn't a typical hangout place for us, but again, I didn't think much of it. I parked my car in the driveway and eagerly approached the house. As I passed by the front window, I saw all my friends watching TV in the living room.

That's when it happened.

I tried to open the front door and walk in, but it was locked. I rang the doorbell. Brandon's older brother answered the door, cracking it slightly, and told me that the guys weren't there. He knew I wasn't an idiot. He knew I could clearly see them through the window and the red Bug in the driveway. But the message was clear: I wasn't welcome. I wasn't part of the group anymore. I was no longer their friend.

> The message was clear: I wasn't welcome. I wasn't part of the group anymore.

I will never forget the feeling in the pit in my stomach as I slowly walked back to the Buick. I glanced at the front window of the house, hoping to look one of them in the eyes and maybe even change his mind. But the blinds had been pulled shut. I couldn't even see inside. They had shut me out completely.

I don't even remember driving home. I was in a state of shock. I sat down on my bed and stared at the wall, and it hit me, all of a sudden...I did not have any friends. I never thought that standing my ground would be so difficult. I kept hoping that one of my friends would be turned off by the party scene and want to spend some time with me. I even had wishful thoughts that this was just a short phase and soon things would return to normal for us and drinking would not even enter the picture. I felt like the stupidest person in the world. I was crushed, rejected and heartbroken. I sat on my bed, staring at the wall, paralyzed.

REAL BAD. REAL FAST.

But the next morning, I tried to get a grip.

"Okay, it's time to toughen up and get over it," I said to myself. I had tons of acquaintances at school. My friends had moved on. So could I. I would make new friends, no big deal.

Unfortunately, things only got worse.

My former friends were ignoring me, but that didn't surprise me. What was surprising was the reaction of other people at my school. All of a sudden, it was like everyone was against me.

The following Monday, I sat with a different group of people at lunch, but they didn't talk to me. Not at all. When I made comments to classmates, they just looked at me and didn't respond. People were even making fun of some of the things I said in class. I was confused and felt very alone.

I soon came to the conclusion that my former friends and I must have been the popular, trend-setting group in our school. It seemed like their new thoughts and feelings toward me sent shock waves throughout the entire school. Before long, it seemed like everyone had a problem with me. I thought hard about the situation. I usually don't overreact about things, but maybe this time, I was just being paranoid. I decided to let it go. It was probably all in my head anyway. It wasn't possible that the whole school hated me.

But it was possible. Eventually, I found out that I was not being paranoid. And, sadly, I soon got some evidence.

First, every year we had Student Council elections. Every year the same students ran for office, and the same ones were elected. I had been class president my freshman, sophomore and junior year. At the end of my junior year, I ran for Class President like I always did. Two others ran against me: Shannah and Josh. Shannah was a responsible girl who always ran against me but never won. Josh was running as a joke, because to him, everything was a joke. He was into drugs and didn't care about anyone or anything. The day of elections, Mrs. Hutchinson, a teacher of mine, called me out of class. She wanted to speak with me privately in the hall.

> Eventually, I found out that I was not being paranoid. And, sadly, I soon got some evidence.

"Joel," she said in a serious tone, "I wanted to let you know before the results were posted, that you were not elected class president this time." I sensed the pity and disbelief in her voice. "I'm so sorry, Joel."

"Wow," I said somberly. "Shannah finally beat me?" I asked.

"Joel," she looked in my eyes, "you came in third."

So, it wasn't all in my head. Now I knew how my classmates really felt about me. Shannah was elected class president our senior year, and even Josh got more votes than I did.

The second proof came during the Winter Homecoming dance. That year the dance was a fundraiser for a charity. It was decided that the senior guy who raised the most money for the charity would be crowned Winter Homecoming King. Well, I raised the most money. At the end of the dance, the results were revealed, and the winner was announced:

"And this year's Winter Homecoming King - Joel Penton!"

There was no applause. Instead, the crowd started to boo.

Yep, I got booed by the entire student body. And it happened as I was being crowned Homecoming King, no less. Nobody was happy for me. Again, I felt completely alone and rejected. There was no longer any doubt. It wasn't just my friends; it was my entire school. I could not believe the price I was paying to keep my commitment. Would it ever be worth it?

WILL IT ALL PAY OFF?

Thankfully, though, I soon got my answer.

While all of this chaos was happening in my personal life, on the field nothing had changed. I was still working hard, committed to being the best football player I could be.

Coach Hood, my football coach, always believed in me. He encouraged me to begin the football recruiting process. I was flattered by his opinion of me, but I didn't have high hopes for a college scholarship. I knew I had improved in high school, and I knew I wanted to keep playing football in college. But I thought my chances at a scholarship were slim. Still, Coach Hood thought it was possible, so I figured I might as well get my name and highlight video out there. Coach Hood made some calls and e-mails to recruiting coaches around the nation for me. A few months into the process, he stopped me in the hallway of my school after lifting one day.

"Joel, I've spoken with a lot of coaches, and it really sounds like you might get a scholarship offer!"

Wow, was it really possible? I was careful not to get my hopes too high, but I knew what I wanted. I *really* wanted to play football in college. After his comment that day, I started to let myself daydream about the future. I thought about where I might go and what it might be like.

But the one place I never let myself dream about was Ohio State. In my mind, Ohio State was unattainable. It wasn't just any college, it wasn't just any team. OSU was THE team. Sure there were other successful football programs across the nation, but for someone who was born and raised in Ohio, everything else was second best.

But, one day Coach Hood was notified that the Ohio State head coach, Jim Tressel, would be stopping by my school! We were surprised, but neither one of us put much thought into his reason for coming.

> But the one place I never let myself dream about was Ohio State.

After all, we hadn't had much contact with the recruiters from Ohio State, just a few e-mails but nothing more. And since we were notified that Coach Tressel was only "stopping by" on his way to see someone else, we were both certain that he wasn't really serious about having me play for the Buckeyes. Still, I was looking forward to meeting him. I hoped to ask him questions about college football and ask his advice.

After only a few minutes in the school, Coach Tressel asked if I would personally show him around. Unbelievable! I was stunned, and I'm sure my face showed it. Coach Tressel's recognizable face generated chatter throughout the entire school. Students and teachers passed by us in the hall, and they looked as surprised as I felt. We began walking to the weight room.

Coach Hood hung back to allow me some time to talk with Coach Tressel one-on-one. I was extremely nervous and didn't know what to say. Coach asked me a little about my hometown and family. I gave him short answers because I was planning on asking him a ton of questions myself. But for some reason, the words would not come out of my mouth, and I couldn't think of anything smart to say. As he continued to ask me questions, my mind was racing with everything I wanted to ask him about college football.

Then, halfway through my frantic thoughts, I zeroed in on his words just in time to hear him say:

"...So I'd like to offer you a full scholarship to Ohio State to play football for the Buckeyes. We think you are Ohio State material."

I clumsily replied, "Great!" I was blown away. At that moment, we entered the weight room, and our wrestling coach approached Coach Tressel with several questions. During their lengthy conversation, I did not add a single word. I was in complete shock. Playing football for Ohio State would be a dream come true. As far as I was concerned, it was out of my league. But then again, there stood Coach Tressel, in the Van Wert High School weight room. My mind was racing.

Did that really just happen? Did he just ask me to play for the Ohio State Buckeyes? That just doesn't happen in real life, does it?

When Coach Tressel left, I turned to Coach Hood and jumped up with a huge smile and yelled, "Can you believe it?" He let out a loud hoot and gave me a huge hug. We started talking excitedly about Ohio State. We were like two kids on Christmas morning.

Our conversation finally ended a couple hours later. I got my clothes and book bag together and walked out to the school parking lot. Ironically, I had taken my mom's white Buick to school that day. As I sat in the car, I reflected on that moment of pure rejection by my friends earlier that year. I thought about the rest of the year and how I felt completely alone.

It was extremely difficult, but I survived. I persevered through some tough times, but ultimately, I accomplished my dream.

I kept my commitment. I stood my ground. And it was all worth it.

MAKING IT PERSONAL

1. Obviously, Joel did a lot of work to get strong and become a good football player. Do you have an area of your life, right now, where you are working that hard? Maybe learning to play an instrument, getting good at a video game, or something else? How much time and energy are you putting into your favorite activity? Why?

    _____

    _____

    _____

2. In high school, Joel experienced serious conflict with his friends. What do you think Joel and his group could have done differently? For example, what might they have done when the first friend (Brandon) started partying? Do you think it would have made a difference?

    _____

    _____

    _____

3. Have you ever been in a situation where a friend (or group of friends) turned on you? What did you do? What advice would you give to someone going through that same struggle?

    _____

    _____

    _____

PART TWO
MAKING
COMMITMENTS
"Take a Stand"

CHAPTER 3:
WHY MAKE COMMITMENTS
"My Three Fake Friends"

So that's my story. I made a big commitment, and I saw it through to the end. And it taught me that keeping your commitments is the best way to find success in life.

Don't believe me? Let me introduce you to my three imaginary friends.

Meet Michael.

Michael *hates* school. To make matters even worse, his girlfriend just broke up with him, and he dreads the thought of seeing her at school with her new boyfriend. No...on second thought, he doesn't care. He has stopped caring. Everything in his life is a mess anyway. His parents are always on his case about the people he hangs out with, he can't stand his 'perfect' sister, and he just wants to move out of the house. He doesn't even have any real friends anymore because people keep stabbing him in the back. He quit the track team and is failing half of his classes.

Michael has tried to make things go his way, but it never works. So why bother?

Enter Evan.

Evan does the bare minimum to get by. He could probably be a really good student, but he just doesn't care enough to work that hard. Besides, he has figured out how to make the system work for him. His parents expect him to get B's and C's, so he does enough to get about an 80%. He never brings a pen or notebook to class because he can always just borrow them from other people. He doesn't take his homework home because he can do about half of it in the hallway before school and the rest right before each class. There are way more interesting things than school to do right now, like music, girls, and video games. Algebra? Come on, what good is X+Y in the real world?

> He has figured out how to make the system work for him.

Evan is a pretty good athlete. He's a starter on the soccer team. But he doesn't get all crazy with the workouts like some of the guys - he's just trying to have some fun. And the future? Well, Evan hasn't gotten that far yet. He figures that he will go to college because that just seems like the next step. He's got plenty of time to get serious and work it all out later.

Welcome Whitney.

Whitney doesn't love school, but she does like the feeling of accomplishment she gets when she does well. She keeps up with all her homework, and even does the extra credit when she needs to. So far, she's earned a 3.95 GPA! She's really good at math and science, and does pretty well at English and Spanish, even though she doesn't really like them as much.

Whitney finally made the basketball team this year. She didn't make the team last year, so she spent the summer working hard, practicing almost every night. She's got a part-time job, too. It's not the greatest pay, but she's saving up for a car. So it's worth it.

And her dreams for the future? She really wants to be accepted to Columbia University and become a dentist like her dad. She'd love to eventually go to work for his dental practice. And she's willing to do what it takes to make that happen.

Michael, Evan, and Whitney. Three totally different people. Three totally different ways to deal with life:

Michael *surrenders*. Life is just too hard. He's stopped caring. He's given up.

Evan *survives*. He's okay with mediocrity. He's just living day to day with no big plans. Whatever happens, happens.

Whitney lives a life of *significance*. She's got a vision for her life that helps her know what to do and why. She's found a path to better herself and the people around her. And she's taking it.

Surrender. Survival. Significance. Why does one person give up while another overcomes? Why does one care so much while another is fine just getting by? Maybe there's nothing wrong with just taking life as it comes…but then again, maybe there's more to life than just getting by.

I know that a lot of people find themselves surrendering or surviving when what they really want is Significance. Maybe you are one of those people. Maybe you see yourself in Michael's story. Maybe you know you are more like Evan. And what you really want is to be more like Whitney. So what do you do?

Is there a way to go from Surrender or Survival to Significance?

Yes, there is. It's called Commitment.

COMMITMENT

Commitment means that you push yourself to rise above your life right now. It means that you dream big and then find ways to achieve those dreams without letting people or feelings or circumstances stop you.

It's a promise you make to yourself that you're going to do better than you ever thought you could. That you're going to do more than others think is possible. That you are going to achieve something great. Something significant.

You want that...right? Who doesn't?

But...

Yeah, I know. This all sounds so perfect when I talk about it like that. Dream big. Do something significant. Blah, Blah, Blah. This "commitment stuff" all sounds so great. But it's not really that easy, is it?

Of course not. If Commitment were easy, everyone would do it. But we don't do it. Instead, we make excuses. Lots of excuses.

So, I'm going to deal with the three most common ones. But I'm not just going to talk about them. I'm going to destroy them. And when I'm done, you won't have these three to use anymore.

I guarantee it.

EXCUSE #1:

"I'm still young, I have lots of time to think about commitments."

Do you remember how, in grade school, waiting for five minutes in the lunch line felt like an hour? Remember how a week of school seemed to take a year? Or how the summer felt like an eternity of fun?

Do you still think time moves slowly? Probably not. For most of us, time seems to fly by. You barely get home on Friday afternoon before it's Monday morning again. An entire school year passes in a blur of football games, school dances, and an occasional homework assignment. One second, junior high is just starting, and the next, you are thinking about college.

Know what I mean?

But in spite of how fast the days seem to fly by, some people go through their entire lives just waiting for "life" to begin. Maybe you are one of those people.

Have you ever thought something like this: "I can't wait to graduate because then my life will really start"? Or this, "When I get my own car things will change"? Or what about, "When I have a job and my own money, everything will be different"?

It's insanely easy to go through life always waiting for the next stage. Always sure things are going to change soon. Always sure that you can wait to get serious about making the right commitments because you have all the time in the world.

Actually, a lot of people do think that. Some spend their entire lives waiting for some magical "right moment" that will make their lives significant. But the time never comes. And they never do anything significant. Like Evan, they simply survive. And life passes them by.

TARGET: EXCUSE #1

Method of Destruction: Re-focus Your Perspective

Be honest. Are you one of these people? Do you really believe that commitments can wait until some future moment or event? Seriously?

The day you were born is the day your life started. Are you breathing? Then you are living right now. And, as obvious as it sounds, the direction you are heading today determines the place where you will someday end up.

Do you really want to be like Evan? One of those people who just lives from day to day without purpose? Not knowing what to do after high school, they go to college. They randomly pick a major. They have a good time for four years, graduate, take the first job offer that comes their way, and live for the weekends. No passion. No goals. Just passing through life.

Do you really want to be that guy? Seriously?!?

Or...would you rather know where you're going and why? Wouldn't you rather pick your college because it has the major you want? Wouldn't it be better to find a job that you are passionate about? Wouldn't it be awesome to look back at your life and see how you chose your own direction?

I once heard a guy say, "If you don't know where you're going, then you'll probably end up somewhere else." You know what? He was totally right. So now it's time to get real.

Are you living like this? Do you wander aimlessly through life and drift about without a firm destination? Have you already arrived at your destination? How would you even know? Do you even know what direction you want to be headed in?

Because, if you don't know, you will absolutely never get there.

44

Think about my life. If I hadn't made a strong commitment to be the best football player I could be, then I wouldn't have been. Simple as that. But I knew where I was going. And that's exactly where I ended up. The same can be true for you.

Some people may live this way, just surviving. But YOU can be different. By making commitments now, you will find yourself with a goal. And you'll be able to see how to get there.

Have you already arrived at your destination? How would you even know?

Remember, your life started the day you were born. You only get one shot at this thing. Don't waste it. Choose a direction. Commit to doing something significant NOW.

EXCUSE #2:

"Commitment sounds boring, I want to have fun."
Some people don't want to make a commitment because they want to LIVE right now. They want to make the most of every minute while they have it. They want to have fun right here, right now.

This group isn't waiting around for a "magic moment" like the last group. Oh no! They're on the opposite side of the field. They have a life packed with "magic moments" already! They are doing, experiencing, enjoying life. They don't have time to make commitments or worry about whether or not what they're doing is really significant.

Maybe you know exactly what I'm describing. Maybe you have a full schedule of parties, practices, and special events that keep your days, evenings, and weekends totally full.

And when I mention Significance, or making commitments, you hear me say something like...

"Okay, you young people, it's time to commit to significance. No more joking around, be serious. Sit up straight, tuck in your shirt. You need to stop going to parties and start studying and practicing every night. Do you want to waste your life in surrender or survival? Of course not! So no more hanging out with friends. No more Facebook. No more texting. No more fun."

And your response: "Hmm...No thanks! See, Joel, it's just that... commitment...well, it's boring. Honestly, just thinking of that word makes me want to take a nap."

Boring? Seriously?!? I don't think so.

TARGET EXCUSE #2
Method of Destruction: Re-define Fun
So, you think commitments are boring? That a life of commitment means not having fun?

Who are you kidding? Look back at my story in Part One.

I made a big commitment, remember? To be the best football player I could be.

Well, look at what happened. I was really bad at first. But I loved the game, and I wanted to be better. So I kept practicing, kept lifting weights, kept learning, kept working to be good, even if it meant missing parties or dances or hanging out with my friends. And the result was a scholarship to Ohio State, a chance to play football on national television, and a National Championship ring.

Was it hard work? Yep. Was it boring? Um...nope.

Was it worth it? Um...lemme think. Yeah...BIG. TIME.

Trust me. Commitment doesn't mean saying good-bye to fun. Commitment means re-defining what "fun" is really all about.

Think of it like a bag of microwave popcorn.

You come home and you're hungry, so you grab a bag of popcorn. But are you going to just start gnawing on the kernels? Not unless you're an idiot. You realize that it's worth another 2 minutes and 37 seconds to wait for the popcorn to pop. Just follow the logic. Sometimes, waiting means getting a much better result than diving in right now.

And that's my point.

Commitment isn't boring and mundane. Living without commitment is boring and mundane. Committing to be the very best actually makes life totally exciting. You're starting to live an adventure. And the rewards are beyond description...especially when you reach your goal.

Okay, I'm not gonna lie. You might have to give up some "fun" things along the way. Everyone who has ever achieved anything had to give up *something*. Of course I hope you don't lose all of your friends like I did. But what you get instead... it's a feeling like nothing else. It's getting first in the long jump after coming in second three years in row. It's beating out the best actor in school for the lead in this year's play. It's scoring your first kiss with the girl of your dreams. Yeah...it's *that* good.

> Commitment isn't boring and mundane. Living without commitment is boring and mundane.

Commitment isn't boring! It can be the start of some of the most exciting moments of your life.

EXCUSE #3:

"Some people are just more ambitious and motivated than others. I'm not an overachiever. I'm just me."

A high school teacher once asked her chatty freshmen to share about some of the commitments they had made in their lives. No one answered. After a long silence, one student finally said, "I have a commitment to *not* do my math homework for the rest of the year."

Wow, that would be funny if it weren't so sad.

"But Joel," you say, "at least that kid made a commitment that he could keep. I mean, all this talk about Significance is great, but I can't make a really good commitment. I'm not good enough. I'll never be able to see it through."

Congratulations! You have now given me Excuse #3.

In a timid, whiny voice, this person says, "Look at all those people who just have 'it.' They get straight A's. They get elected class president. They always do the extra credit. They have it all, they get it all, they know it all. Nothing stops them...but *me*? I'm just me. I can't do what they do. So why even try?"

Really?!?

Are you really trying to tell me that you can't make a commitment because you've never been elected president of your class? That commitments are only for people who have some secret that gives them some kind of "overachiever super-power"?

It's Not About starting out great. It's About becoming great.

Is this your excuse? You see the high expectations that others set for themselves, and you get discouraged. You've been look-

48

ing at the "overachievers" and are convinced that, if you can't live up to the same standards, it's not even worth trying.

But are you right? Nope.

There is no secret to making (and reaching) your commitment. Trust me. It's not about starting out great. It's about becoming great.

TARGET: EXCUSE #3

Method of Destruction: Re-Examine Yourself

Let's be honest here. This excuse just doesn't make any sense, does it? Commitments can't be just for people who have it all together already. Because no matter what it looks like, nobody *really* has it all together. And absolutely nobody starts out having it all together.

Do you really think Bill Gates knew Microsoft would be the huge success it is when he started the company?

Do you really think Oprah Winfrey felt capable of becoming the most influential woman in entertainment when she got her first on-air job at age 17?

Do you really think that Brad Pitt or Julia Roberts guessed they'd be internationally famous when they got their first movie role?

Sorry to disappoint you. That's just not how it works. Everybody, even an overachiever, has to start somewhere.

Just think about it. An "overachiever" is someone who *achieves above or beyond what is expected*. They *over*-achieve. They do more than anyone expected they could do. They're just ordinary people who work hard. People who made a commitment to be or do something. And they stick with it. No matter what.

So what if you don't feel qualified to make a commitment? Qualified has nothing to do with it. I certainly wasn't qualified to earn a spot on the Ohio State Buckeyes Football team. Not at first anyway.

Your commitment is not about living up to someone else. It's about pursuing what YOU want most out of life. With all that you've got until you reach the goal.

So what DO you want? When you're totally honest with yourself, what would you like to achieve?

Maybe it's *huge*, like a cure for cancer or world peace.
Maybe it's *personal*, like a good education or a great-paying career or national recognition.
Maybe it's a *thing*, like being able to buy a car or an iPod or a designer dress.
Maybe it's a little more *everyday*, like getting an A in math or a date with the quarterback.

What other people do isn't really important. What other people want to accomplish isn't the point. What matters is doing what you want to do, becoming who you want to be.

And the best thing you can be is YOURSELF. You are only responsible for your goals, your commitments, your focus. You have certain strengths, gifts, and desires that can help you be successful. The trick is to know what they are and commit to becoming the best you can be. And when that happens, trust me...you'll be the one they call "overachiever."

MICHAEL, EVAN AND WHITNEY -
Two Years After High School Graduation
So you really think your excuses are still good enough to keep you from making a commitment? Are you still sure that a life of surrender or survival is enough to satisfy you for the rest of your life?

Maybe we should check back in with our three friends from the beginning of the chapter...

Remember Michael? He managed to graduate from high school, barely. He has a job at a video store, but since the pay's not great, he lives in his parents' basement. Still no girlfriend, so he spends most of his time playing video games.

How about Evan? He went to USC because a lot of his friends were going there. His parents are paying half of his tuition, and student loans are covering the rest. He finally declared a major last semester. He still has no plans for after college, but between weekend parties and his new girlfriend, he's having a great time.

> He still has no plans for after college, but between weekend parties and his new girlfriend, he's having a great time.

And Whitney? She graduated with a 3.9 GPA and was accepted to Columbia. She's using scholarships and student loans to cover her tuition. Some of her classes are pretty tough, but she found a tutor to help her keep her grades up, especially in Chemistry. And she's been volunteering at the University dental clinic which has gotten her some great experience for the real world.

WHY MAKE COMMITMENTS?

So today, where are you? Surrendering? Surviving? Wishing for Significance?

Making commitments is the way to avoid a life of surrender or survival. It's the first step on the road to somewhere. The excuses not to do it are there. We can latch on to any or all of them and remain exactly where we are.

Or...

We can start to move on. We can embrace commitment as the path towards Significance.

I am convinced that understanding this one concept can change your life permanently. It is what changed mine.

Think back to the first chapter. You've read my story. You know how I made my commitment to be the best football player I could be. I took my dad's challenge, got out of bed, and did push-ups until I was exhausted. And then I pursued that goal until I achieved it.

But why? Why, as a seventh grader, did I do any of that?

Because I realized that I wanted my life to count for something. I wanted to have a story to tell. I wanted to look back and see how far I'd come and know that I'd been the best I could be - that my actions and decisions had purpose.

So the question that remains is a simple one: What about your life? Are you willing to embrace commitment as the road that leads away from survival and surrender and towards Significance? Are you ready to start the journey toward something spectacular, something bigger than you can imagine right now?

Making a commitment is the first step. Look one last time at our three examples...

MICHAEL, EVAN AND WHITNEY -
Now
Michael is still in his parents' basement, but the video store closed, and he hasn't been able to find another job yet. Still no girlfriend. And he's still playing video games. Five years ago it was fun. Three years ago it was funny. Now it's just sad.

After five years at USC, Evan still didn't get his degree. His parents stopped paying for school after his junior year, and his student loans got so high that he had to drop out and get a job to pay them off. He's still kind of hoping to finish later, but for now, he's just putting in his 40 hours at the call center to cover his bills. He used to just survive his classes and have fun. Now he's trying to survive in the real world. And it's not so fun anymore.

Whitney graduated with honors from Columbia. She is engaged to the guy she started dating last year. He used to be her chemistry tutor. Right now, she's working at her dad's dental practice, paying off her student loans and getting experience. But she also has a new dream. She's hoping to open her own dental clinic in an urban area of town to provide good dental care to underprivileged children. She's got a plan in place, and she's looking forward to the day her dream becomes a reality.

> Now he's trying to survive in the real world. And it's not so fun anymore.

SO WHAT ABOUT YOU?

So, do you want to be like Michael? Evan? Whitney?

I hope you said Whitney. I hope you are ready to pursue Significance. And I hope you see that the secret to Significance is making commitments.

When I was in seventh grade, my dad challenged me to be the best I could be. So that's the challenge I'm offering to you, too. Start today. Be willing to put off some 'fun' now for even bigger rewards later. Don't worry about setting your expectations too high.

Make the commitment that will change your life. You won't regret it. I guarantee it. And if you asked them, I bet our three friends would agree with me.

MAKING IT PERSONAL

1. Think about the three "fake friends" mentioned in this chapter. Describe each one below in your own words.

    Michael: _____

    Evan: _____

    Whitney: _____

2. Do you think you are like one of these three? Are you like one of them in some areas and a different one in other areas? Explain.

    _____

    _____

    _____

3. Excuse #1 said "I have plenty of time to make commitments, I'm young." Why do you think that adults are always telling teens to 'start making the right choices NOW'? Are they right? What do you think would help convince teens to make good decisions now?

    _____

    _____

    _____

4. Do you think that "Commitments = Boring" (Excuse #2)? Joel argues that "keeping your commitments = the most fun ever." Do you agree or disagree? Why?

    _____

    _____

    _____

5.   The final excuse (#3) was "I'm not an overachiever."
     What qualities do you think are really necessary for a
     person to achieve great things?

_____

_____

_____

CHAPTER 4:
HOW TO MAKE COMMITMENTS
"The Timid Trombone Player"

How hard could it be to sell 20 raffle tickets for the Fall Home-coming football game?

Next to impossible, that's how hard.

Just ask Sara, a sophomore trombone player in the high school marching band. She was too shy to approach anyone about buying a ticket. But she was also too timid to tell the band director she couldn't meet the "Sell 20 Tickets Challenge."

Luckily she had an idea that wouldn't draw any unnecessary attention to herself. She bought all 20 tickets herself. Problem solved!

At half-time Sara performed on the field with the rest of the band. Being in a group was fine...she just hated to be singled out. Before their final song, the announcer drew the winning raffle ticket. Everyone waited in anticipation to see who had won. The ticket was drawn, and the name was read...

"Congratulations... Sara Penton!"

Sara hung her head, too embarrassed to look up. The announcer continued, "And...I think she is that trombone player slouched over on the 45 yard line. Come on Sara, wave to the crowd!" The people in the stands burst into laughter.

It was one of the most humiliating moments of her life.

My older sister Sara was always a sensitive, sweet girl. And she was, obviously, a big-time introvert. But she's also incredibly smart. Early in high school, she was already thinking about college. She wanted to have the best education possible with the limited resources available to her. She wanted to do something special. That had always been her personal commitment.

So, during her junior year, Sara began to research colleges. She went to the library, researched online, and spoke to the school counselor.

Clearly, a degree from an Ivy League school would be very impressive, and with her grades and test scores, she would probably be accepted. But there was a problem. She couldn't afford the tuition, and scholarships would not be enough. So she had to consider other options.

How could she get an Ivy League education, but without the cost?

Soon, she discovered one possible, but very challenging, solution to her problem - a military academy. The military academies provided the same quality education as an Ivy League school, but for free! After a little more research and a couple of visits, Sara decided on a specific goal - to be accepted to the United States Naval Academy.

Sara knew, however, that getting in would be the greatest challenge she had faced in her life.

She began by breaking down her goal into smaller steps. There were three major areas in which Sara had to prove her worth to the Academy: physical, political and academic. In the area of academics, she knew she wouldn't have much of a problem. The other two areas, however, were a different story.

Why?

Well, let me explain something briefly about the Naval Academy. A typical applicant has a family with a military background, is an athlete, and is usually an outspoken leader at their high school with dozens of extra-curricular activities.

Sara didn't fit that mold. At. All.

Sara only had two extra-curricular activities: Band and German Club. And she was one of the quietest kids at school. For any other school, this wouldn't have been a problem. But for the Naval Academy, it was. A huge problem. See, applicants to the Academy had to get a nomination from a congressman. And there was no way that a congressman would nominate someone who wouldn't even open her mouth to sell raffle tickets. Sara had to get her name out there. She had to interview important political figures in her town.

> Sara only had two extra-curricular activities: Band and German Club.

She had a real challenge ahead of her.

And wait, I'm not done. Remember that I said a typical applicant is also an athlete? Well, Sara was not an athlete. In fact, she tried out for the high school softball team and got cut. But now she was applying to a school with specific requirements for physical fitness. A 1.5 mile time-tested run? A required number of 'real' push-ups (not the girlie kind!) and sit-ups in two minutes? No way. Sara wasn't even close.

Not only did she have all of these factors against her, but she also knew that only 10% of the applicants accepted to the Naval Academy were female.

Was it even possible? Would she totally be wasting her time?

Sara chose to not freak out about those questions. Instead she came up with a plan. She had decided this was the direction she wanted to go. The Naval Academy was her choice for a good education. So she went for it. No looking back. No losing focus.

She knew she would have to begin pursuing the congressional nomination right away. She made a list of the main three things she needed to do.

- Practice mock interviews until she felt comfortable.
- Interview influential political figures.
- Get letters of recommendation from the right people.

"There!" She thought to herself, "That's not too bad." She immediately began the process *that day* by setting up a mock interview with a neighbor.

She also knew she needed to begin working out ASAP. But she had *no clue* of where to begin. Sara quickly looked up the requirements for the Naval Academy fitness assessment. She decided that it would be best to give these requirements to a personal trainer and hire him to train her.

Using the money she'd made working all summer at a drug store, she joined a gym and found the best trainer she could afford. After looking at the requirements and then skeptically looking at Sara, he said, "Okay, we need to start next Monday." Sara was shocked and a little scared to have to begin so soon. But then she thought about the Naval Academy and how much she wanted to get in. "Okay, I'll be here."

Finally, after months of waiting, working, and wondering if she was crazy, it was winter of her senior year. Sara submitted her application to the Naval Academy. By this time, she was physically stronger and more fit, confident, and outspoken. As she waited to hear from the Academy, Sara knew that the experience had changed her life for the better, even if she didn't get accepted.

But she did. My sister Sara made it into one of the most prestigious universities in the country. She was going to the United States Naval Academy!

Sara's first year at the Naval Academy was even tougher than the process she went through to get in. It beat her down, but she learned how to be mentally tough. Her steadfast work ethic and emphasis on keeping her commitments was again challenged. She pushed through and gained more and more confidence each year.

By the time she was a senior, she set a new challenge for herself. She decided to apply for one of the top leadership positions in the Naval Academy.

And, yeah, she got it.

Not only was she going to graduate from of one of the best universities in the nation, but now, only 12 people in the whole Academy had a higher rank than her! She was the new Commander of the Naval Academy Drum and Bugle Corps (that's a fancy name for the school's marching band).

In the fall of her senior year, Sara arranged for the Drum and Bugle Corps to stop at our hometown on their way to play at a big football game against Notre Dame. She timed it up so that they were able to play at a Friday night Van Wert High School football game.

As she led the Corps onto the field at halftime, she looked up at the stands and couldn't help but think of that embarrassing raffle ticket night. She almost laughed out loud as she thought about how humiliated she had felt all those years before. She took her place and waited for the announcer. This time she wasn't embarrassed at all by what he had to say...

"Conductor and Commander of the Naval Academy Drum and Bugle Corps...please welcome back...Sara Penton!"

PREGAME - BEFORE YOU COMMIT

Well, here we finally are...the moment of truth. So far, you've read my story and my sister Sara's story. You know why I think it's important to make commitments in your own life.

Are you still with me? Good. Because now, I'd like to take things one step further.

See, we've all made little commitments along the way, like earning enough money to buy something we really wanted. But now I'm challenging you to take it to the next level. I'm talking about making a serious, life-changing kind of commitment.

But...

You may be wondering, "Commitments and Significance all sound great, Joel. But how do I actually MAKE a commitment?"

I'm so glad you asked.

PREGAME WARMUP #1: *Consider your Passions and Strengths*

For most of my high school years, I excelled at a sport other than football — wrestling.

I gotta admit, I was pretty good at it. And it came naturally. Many of my fellow wrestlers were totally focused on wrestling. It was their main sport, so they went to summer camps and spent much of their off-season time preparing for meets. But I was a different story.

See, I joined the wrestling team to help me get stronger and keep in shape for football. And it worked. But I found out that I was actually good at it, too. I ended up placing 3rd at the State

Championship my junior year and had the best record in my high school's history. My wrestling abilities surprised a lot of people, including me!

So why am I telling you this? Because I want to pump myself up even more than I already have? Actually, no. I want to make a point:

The first step in making a commitment is to discover your passions and your strengths.

Think about it this way: Strengths are what you're good at. Passions are what you love. For me, wrestling was a *strength*. I was good at it, and I enjoyed it, but I didn't love it the way I loved football. Football was a *passion*. I loved it, but I had to work for a long, long time before it became a strength. But I never had to choose between them. I did both.

And that's my point. Passions and Strengths work together. It doesn't have to be one or the other. You need to consider both areas, because when you do, I can almost guarantee that you will find the commitment you were meant to make.

So what are your passions and strengths? Not sure? Well, the best way to start figuring it out is to ask yourself two questions and write down the answers that come to mind.

1. What Passions would you love to pursue?

You've lived enough life to know some things that you really like to do. What do you daydream about during history class? What would you

If someone gave you $50, what would you spend it on?

do every day if you could? If someone gave you $50, what would you spend it on? A video game or sheet music or art supplies or a new iPod? These are your passions...write them down.

2. What Strengths can you build on?

What are you good at right now? What natural talents, gifts, and abilities do you have? (And yes, everybody has some.) Can you create new recipes or play music by ear? Have you always been told you were naturally good at soccer? Maybe you speak well in public. Maybe you have always been good at handling money. Or good at math. Or good at writing databases. Nothing is too small to fit into this category. If you can do it, it counts. So write it down.

Now...read your lists again. What jumps out at you? Be honest. What one thing in these two categories really gets you excited, more than any of the others?

That is your answer. That is where you need to focus. That is the beginning, the starting point, for making your commitment.

PREGAME WARMUP #2: *Comprehend the Definition (of Commitment)*

Okay, so you've got a general idea for a commitment. Good. Now it's time to think about what it really means to make a commitment.

"I know, it's kind of like a New Year's resolution." Um...no. Not even close.

Think about New Year's resolutions for a second. People talk for days about what they're going to start doing or stop doing or blah, blah, blah. But does it happen? Usually not. For most people, the resolution has died before January even ends. They just don't seem to be able to carry through on their "resolution." So why does this happen? Every year? Over and over again?

I say it's because what most people make on New Year's Day isn't really a resolution. It's a wish. They aren't resolving to be different. They are hoping to be different. They are wishing they were different. And a wish is not a commitment.

Resolve is a serious word. It's about determination. Being steadfast. Being firm. That's why I'm saying that New Year's "resolutions" aren't commitments. A resolution, an actual commitment, is for real. It's intentional. It means you're taking a stand.

And here's the thing: *When you make a commitment, the kind that leads to Significance, you cannot simply be wishing for something you aren't willing to work hard to achieve.* You have to clearly describe your goal as a commitment.

Look at my sister, Sara. Sara decided to apply to the Naval Academy. But it wasn't just an "I hope I get in" sort of application process. She was clear about what she needed to do. She was specific about the areas that she needed to address. She had the academics, but she needed to work hard to become more outgoing and more physically fit.

> A resolution, an actual commitment, is for real. It's intentional. It means you're taking a stand.

So what about you?

Does your commitment sound something like: "Oh, it would be really nice to get the lead part in this year's school play"? Be honest. Is that what you're calling your commitment? Because that is not going to work. That is not a commitment; it's a wish. Instead, you have to say, "I am going to do whatever I can do to get the lead role in this year's school play." That is firm. That is resolve. That is a commitment. And, that is what I'm talking about.

This is a lesson that I learned the hard way.

In 8th grade, I began working out with the HS football team. I remember one afternoon very clearly. Coach said to me, "Joel, I see you working hard in the weight room, and I hope you have some serious goals that you want to achieve." I confidently replied, "Yeah, I want to get a football scholarship and be valedictorian." And I did. For real. I wanted to graduate with straight A's.

Now you're thinking, "That's funny, Joel, you haven't mentioned that commitment yet. You've only talked about your football stuff. How come?"

Because I never actually made that second commitment. When it came to football, I had made a real commitment. I thought it through. I pictured my success and considered what I might have to sacrifice. I took clear steps in the right direction. I had a plan.

But being valedictorian was more like a wish. It sounded cool. But I hadn't thought it through. I hadn't pictured my success and considered my sacrifices. I had no plan. And as a result, I had no commitment. Once I entered high school, the quarters rolled by, and I settled for the occasional B. I soon began to accept that my dream would not become a reality. And I had only myself to blame.

Boo Hoo. Sad story, I know. But honestly, what I went through to reach my football commitment was a small price to pay for the success I got. And had I known then what I know now, I would have made another difficult, but rewarding, commitment to academics. But I didn't; I let it stay a wish. And my wish did not come true. But my commitment, my real resolution, did.

The same is going to be true for you. Your commitment has to be a real resolution, not a wish, or there's no way you'll see it through.

GAME TIME - MAKE YOUR COMMITMENT

So, here we are. You are ready to really make your commitment.

You've found your passions and considered your strengths. You've thought about the details of your commitment. It's not just a wish; you know exactly what you want to be. And now... it's time.

Like my sister applying to the Naval Academy, you are totally committed. No turning back. No losing focus.

But what do you do next?

PLAY OPTION #1: *Get It Out*

When I made my commitment to football, I was serious. I was going to do everything in my power to be the best football player I could be. But no one knew about it but me. I was by myself there in my room, on the floor doing push-ups. If I gave up or changed my mind, who would know? I could just not do it, and no one would even notice.

> If I gave up or changed my mind, who would know? I could just not do it, and no one would even notice.

I knew if my commitment just stayed as a thought in my head, it would die a quick death. I'd never see it through. So I needed to get it out. Out of my head. Out of my hands. Out into the world.

And you need to do the same.

"Sure, Joel. Sounds great. Um...how?"

First, write it down. Try putting an actual copy of your commitment where you can see it every day. Do I mean like, tape it to the wall? Yep. That's exactly what I mean. It's something that worked really well for me.

I remember writing out goals at least twice a year. I would do it during class, usually. I mounted these goals on the wall of my basement workout room. I replaced the old goals with new ones, and I was able to be reminded of my goal almost every day. Whenever I rested in between sets, I would look up at the wall where my goal was written. There it was staring me in the face. Challenging me. Inspiring me.

By keeping my goal in front of me, literally, visually, it was way easier to stay motivated.

You might do better with a journal or blog. Or you could tape it to your mirror. Or make it your desktop background. You can put it anywhere you want, but the more often you see it, the better. What's important is that it's out of your head, where you can see it.

Second, try telling someone. If your commitment stays in your head, it's easy to cop out. But when you make it public, there is no turning back. Once you've said it out loud, to someone else, your commitment will suddenly become more real. And you'll be more motivated to see it through. So tell someone.

Remember, the longer your commitment stays inside your heart and your head, the easier it will be for you to get lazy and let it slip away. So get it out there.

PLAY OPTION #2: *Cut it Up*

When Sara made her commitment to get into the Naval Academy, she started by making a plan.

She first broke her goal down into three smaller goals: academics, politics, and physical fitness. Then she broke each of those three down into even smaller goals. She couldn't "get fit" on her own. So she got a trainer who walked her through the process. She couldn't just go get a congressional recommendation. But she could practice doing interviews and start getting her name out. The big goal was overwhelming. But by breaking it down into pieces, she was able to keep moving forward until she found herself exactly where she wanted to go.

And that is true, no matter what the goal is.

Think about building a house, for example. You could never just "build a house" without a plan and specific goals that need to be accomplished to achieve that plan. The foundation is always dug first. The plumbing has to be run before the sinks can go in. Walls have to be finished before windows can be put in. You see my point, right?

If you want your commitment to really stick, you have to have a plan. You need to break your commitment down into smaller goals.

> I knew I couldn't just make one big goal that said, "Be the best."

When I made my commitment for football, I knew it wouldn't happen overnight. A lot of steps separated the youth league no-cut team from the Ohio State Buckeyes. I knew I couldn't just make one big goal that said, "Be the best." I needed to have some realistic smaller goals to climb that mountain.

My first small goal was to increase my strength. I was tall and wimpy. I got pushed all over the field. I needed to be stronger, so I decided to make "50 push-ups" my first goal. I worked and worked and did push-ups every night on my bedroom floor. For days I would give up just short of 50, pathetically sucking air while laying on the carpet. But finally, I was able to do 50 push-ups in a row. And I kept going. Soon, I could do 75 push-ups. Then 100.

Had I reached my final goal? No. But with each small goal, I kept moving one step closer.

And what about you? Maybe you want to become a veterinarian or a graphic designer or a lawyer, not a better football player. Doesn't matter. Regardless of your overall goal, you'll still need to break it down into small steps.

Make your plans *personal*, so you'll want to achieve them. Make them as *specific* as possible. Put them into practice *as soon as* possible. And make sure they are *progressive*, moving you a little bit closer to your goal with each step.

Have a plan. Break your commitment into smaller goals.

Sara reached her goal this way. So did I. And so can you.

POST GAME CELEBRATION

So, you did it, right? You've made your commitment? You've taken a stand? Excellent.

Of course, there is still a lot of work to do before you reach that goal. The next section deals with how to Stand Your Ground. Having faith in yourself. How to fight for your commitments. How much you need friends. And how to deal with failure.

Let me tell you, the road to your commitment will be one wild ride! But it's also worth every second. Let's dive in...

MAKING IT PERSONAL

Pregame Questions

1. Think about your passions. Is there anything you absolutely love to do, even if you might not be that good at it? Make a list of your passions in the space below.

    _____

    _____

    _____

2. Think about your strengths. What are the things you are really good at? What are the things that people ask you to do for them? Remember, nothing is too small to go on this list. Write down your strengths in the space provided.

    _____

    _____

    _____

3. Not everything you want to do is really a commitment (like Joel's 'wish' to become valedictorian). Do you have any 'wishes' that aren't really commitments? They might start off as thoughts that sound like this, "man, it would be pretty cool if…" Write them down.

    _____

    _____

    _____

Game Time Questions: Making Your Commitment

4.   Go back to your lists of passions and strengths in Question 1. Take some time to think about what commitments you *could* make for each of the passions or strengths you just listed. Write down some of your ideas below. (Remember, there are no "wrong" ideas.)

_____

_____

_____

5.   Pick the one potential commitment that speaks to you most. Write that idea below. Be sure to word it as a firm commitment, not just a wish. Feel free to revise it until it says just what you want it to say. This is your Commitment.

_____

_____

_____

6.   Write the final version in the space provided. Then sign your name.

_____

_____

_____

7.   Joel found it helpful to put his commitment where he could see it and to tell someone. Do you think these two small things are important? Where could you post your commitment so it was always in front of you? Who might you tell about your commitment?

_____

_____

_____

8.   Remember how Sara "cut up" her commitment into smaller goals like practicing mock interviews? You need to start there, too. Write down the first step you need to take to start towards your goal. Give some details. How long do you want to give yourself to complete this goal? What exactly will you need to do to reach this smaller goal?

_____

_____

_____

9.   Write down other steps you know you'll need to take in order to reach your goal. Don't be afraid to break them down or rearrange them as you go. Make them as detailed as possible so you can easily tell when you've completed them.

_____

_____

_____

PART THREE
KEEPING
COMMITMENTS
"Stand Your Ground"

CHAPTER 5:

FAITH

"Crazy Chris"

"Fight the team across the field...show them Ohio's here..."

The locker room erupted in loud booing and heckling as we sang. I mean LOUD booing.

Come on, we were just freshman, and it was our first day on The Ohio State Football team. How were we expected to know all the words of the school's legendary fight song? We certainly didn't know that we'd have to sing it together as a freshman class in front of the whole team at the first team meeting. Apparently, it was a tradition they did every year during the first night of preseason camp. That year, it was our turn.

After the humiliation, we were handed a camp schedule and a large binder called the 'Winners Manual,' a collection of wisdom, advice, and other truths compiled by Coach Tressel. We were introduced to our new teammates and coaches, then Coach went over some team policies. He closed the night with a few inspirational and motivational words from the Manual. His final bit of advice was, "Get some rest tonight, because tomorrow *you'll need it.*" As we headed back to the hotel, I thought to myself, "It can't be *that* hard. I've been working hard all summer. This won't be so bad."

I was wrong.

The next morning began with a RUDE awakening: loud pounding on our hotel door at 6 a.m. We quickly got of bed, rushed
through breakfast, and
hiked to our nearby
training facility, affec-
tionately called 'The
Woody', after legendary
OSU coach Woodrow
"Woody" Hayes. After

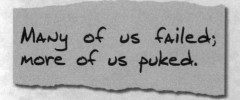

Many of us failed;
more of us puked.

throwing on our workout clothes, we walked as a team about
a mile to the stadium. What followed was an excruciating conditioning test. Twenty sprints across the field and back, each
in under 21 seconds, with only 30 seconds rest in between. If
we failed at any point, we were expected to repeat the sprints
periodically throughout camp until we passed. As freshmen,
we didn't exactly know how to pace ourselves. As a big lineman, I had never had to sprint like that before. Many of us
failed; more of us puked. It sucks to have two rude awaken-
ings in one day.

After the conditioning test, we went in for a team meeting, then
separated into offense and defense for a second meeting. We
broke down even further into position groups for yet another
meeting. Were we ever going to *actually* play football? Finally
we took the field for our first 2-hour practice of the day, which
I must say went pretty well. We seemed to be doing well as a
team and working together easily.

As soon as practice concluded, we headed inside to watch
some film. I sat in the classroom with my fellow d-linemen
and watched footage of a team that looked horrible. They
were disorganized, lazy, and just plain incompetent. Before
long, though, I recognized my own jersey on our practice field.
When I finally figured out that this was *our* practice from just a
few minutes before, I was so embarrassed at my performance
that I wanted to leave the room and hide in a closet. I looked

around at the other guy's faces, and it seemed like they were just as humiliated.

Wow. We had a lot of work to do if we were going to become The Ohio State Buckeyes that everyone knew and loved. Weight lifting came next for about an hour, then finally lunch together as a team. Yes, it was only *lunch time*! After lunch, we were granted an hour to rest at the hotel, which seemed to end as soon as I laid down on the bed. That was yet another rude awakening. Then we walked the long mile back to the Woody for another meeting with our position groups, to watch the rest of that film with those idiots on the field.

Around 3 p.m. we started our second practice, and immediately following, we watched the video of that practice. Finally, we slumped across the street to dinner at our hotel. But the day wasn't over yet! Still one last meeting, then finally we were sent to our hotel rooms to sleep for the night.

That schedule may sound grueling, but almost every team in the country follows a similar routine in pursuit of greatness. Two things, however, made us special, different from the rest. It was the start of our day and the end of our day that set us apart.

The first meeting of each day was always the same. We would break out the 'Winners Manual' and have something Coach Tressel called 'quiet time.' The Winners Manual was a big binder that contained sections on the 15 "Fundamentals of a Winner." Each day we focused on a different fundamental, like hard work, humility, discipline, faith, excellence, etc. Then we spent the next 15 or 20 minutes in reflective thought and silence. When everyone was finished, Coach would ask if anyone wanted to share something they learned from the Manual that impacted them. Players raised their hands one by one to mention a poem, quote, or story that was inspirational to them. Sometimes our comments brought about further explanation from Coach Tressel or in-depth conversations with fellow team-mates. It was always inspiring or motivating.

The way we ended our day was also special. I loved our last meeting of the day. Most teams in the country would take the opportunity to talk more about football, perhaps watch even more film or talk about strategy. Not us. At our final meeting, we didn't talk about football at all. We talked about life.

The meeting was led by our seniors who took turns sharing their wisdom. They would talk about their lives and the things that they had learned at Ohio State. They shared with us their favorite OSU traditions, their heroes, and stories from their childhood. Each senior would then tell the team the one Fun-damental from the 'Winners Manual' that he believed the team needed the most to be successful that year. As a freshman, I was absolutely stunned by what the seniors had to say. Over half of the seniors picked the exact same fundamental to share with the team. Nearly all of them said that what we needed that year to be successful was FAITH.

Wait...FAITH? Really?

I'll never forget one of the senior's speeches. The guy's name was Chris Conwell, and he was a defensive back from Youngstown. Like most of the others, he went up front and said that the one thing we needed this year to succeed was faith. Then he said IT.

"Guys, I *know* that we are going to win the National Champion-ship this year, guys, I do not see us losing."

I almost laughed out loud. I sat there as a freshman thinking, "Who is this guy? He's crazy. We aren't even ranked in the pre-season top 10. We aren't supposed to make it to one of the top bowl games. We haven't even played a single game yet! How can he be so sure?"

KEEPING COMMITMENTS "FAITH"

Several weeks later, we started out our season with a huge game against Texas Tech. The media "experts" said it would be a close game. We killed them. After the game, we sang our fight song as a team in the locker room to celebrate our victory. A week later, after another win, I found myself singing the fight song again. And the next week. We kept playing and kept winning. The media was surprised. I was surprised.

> I sat there as a freshman thinking, "Who is this guy? He's crazy."

As I was getting ready for practice at The Woody one day, I happened to run into Chris Conwell. We talked about school, life, and football. He said, "Joel, you'll have a great career here, because after this year you will have your National Championship ring and you will go on to win other Championships and do other things..." Again I thought, "What is he talking about?" He acted like it was a done deal. He talked like winning the Championship was going to happen for sure. It was one thing to dream big during a motivational speech in front of our whole team at the beginning of the year, but this just seemed delusional! Chris was just dropping comments into casual conversation about winning the National Championship as if it was guaranteed.

But it wasn't just Chris. All of the seniors had the same plan that year. They had made a commitment to win the National Championship, and they all had faith that it would happen. As the season went on, we would pull out a win when the odds were against us. We won some extremely close games that we were not predicted to win. Everyone else was surprised by our continuous winning; our seniors were not.

The season's defining moment came in an away game against Purdue. Purdue was tough that year, and the game was back and forth all night long. When we reached the 4th quarter, we trailed 6-3, having not yet scored a touchdown. With just a few minutes left, we got the ball and had to drive the length of the field to score a touchdown for the win or kick a field goal for the tie. It was a daunting task. At mid-field with just 2 minutes left, we came to a huge 4th and 1 play. If we failed to gain at least 1 yard on this play, Purdue would get the ball back, run the clock out, and we would lose. Everyone assumed our quarterback, Craig Krenzel, would keep the ball and run up the middle to gain the 1 yard we needed to get a first down and keep the drive alive.

However, he did something completely unexpected.

Craig dropped back and threw a long pass to Michael Jenkins in the end zone. Touchdown, Buckeyes! The dream of a National Championship was still alive. As the teams were leaving the field, the media flocked to Craig. With bright lights shining in his eyes and cameras in his face, they asked him, "It was crazy out there. When did you know that you guys were going to win?" He casually replied,

"I knew we were going to win as soon as I let go of the ball."

Craig, one of our team leaders, reminded me yet again of the composed and steadfast faith the seniors embraced all year long.

After winning a double-overtime victory against Illinois in the freezing cold, we played Michigan at home to earn the right to play in the National Championship game. The battle with the Wolverines came down to the last play. And what do you know, with a final score of 14-9 the underrated, Cinderella Buckeyes were set to contend for the National Title.

In the weeks of preparation before the Bowl game, it was impossible to tune out the murmurings of the sports media world. We were going to play Miami of Florida who had just won the National Title the year before. People were saying that we didn't have a chance, and that we were going to get killed. Many sports fanatics said that it was silly to even try to play Miami, that the Buckeyes should not even show up because that would be less embarrassing for us. Conversely, the team atmosphere at practice was absolutely undaunted. I did not sense even a hint of doubt or fear in our senior leaders. They were consistently encouraging and upbeat.

> People were saying that we didn't have a chance, and that we were going to get killed.

You see, the plan was never to win the public's confidence. The plan was to win the National Championship. So far, everything was going according to plan.

The night of the game arrived. Like many of our games that year, the score went back and forth down to the final seconds of the game. We even went into overtime, a common scene for us that year. At the end of overtime, we had one last play to score a touchdown to tie the game and force a second overtime. Once again, we were in a position where any mistake at this point would cost us the win. Craig dropped back to pass. This time his pass fell incomplete, and Miami fans exploded in celebration. Fireworks went off, and the players began to celebrate on the field. We had fallen short by one play. But wait — there was a penalty flag on the field! The game wasn't over! We had another chance! Buckeye fans went insane. Miami fans fell into silent shock. After a quick score to tie the game, we were heading into double overtime.

We got the ball first and scored a touchdown. Miami got the ball and drove all the way down to the 1 yard line. We kept them out of the end zone for 2 more plays. Now it was 4th and 1, their chance to tie or lose on this one play. Miami's final pass fell incomplete. This time there weren't any flags on the field.

Game over.

The Buckeyes had clinched the National Championship! There were fireworks, confetti, and complete chaos. Swarms of Buckeye fans and media flooded the field. A stage was quickly set up on the 50-yard-line, and National Championship hats and shirts were handed out to the team. Coach Tressel and the seniors gathered together on the stage for the award ceremony. The National Championship trophy was presented to Coach Tressel, and he carefully lifted the Crystal Football off of the trophy and kissed it. He passed it to his senior team members who also kissed it. I stood in the midst of my teammates, watching the scene in disbelief. I looked up at the sky with the fireworks exploding above us and the confetti falling down on us, and all I could think of was one thing: Chris Conwell.

I thought about his remarks in the preseason camp evening meeting. I thought about his casual comments to me. I couldn't stop thinking about his faith.

When we finally made it back into the locker room after the game, we reflected on our commitment to win a National Championship. Despite all the opposition, we pressed on with unwavering faith and now we had attained our goal: we were National Champions. There was only one thing left to do. We stood up and ended the season just how it had started; we proudly sang our school fight song, this time knowing all the words because we had LIVED them:

"Fight the team across the field show them Ohio's Here,
Set the earth reverberating with the mighty cheer rah rah rah,

Hit them hard and see how they fall,
Never let that team have the ball,
Hail, hail, the gang's all here so let's win that old conference now."

FAITH... REALLY!?!

Now you may be thinking, "Okay Joel, that's a great story, but seriously...Faith? Isn't "faith" just some religious thing? It doesn't really matter in my life, does it? And it's not like it always works anyway. Didn't the other team have faith too? But they lost. So what exactly are you talking about?"

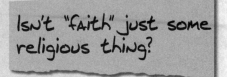

Isn't "faith" just some religious thing?

I am so glad you asked. I know that talking about "faith" can be a little confusing. So let me start with exactly those questions.

Isn't "faith" just some religious thing? Well, it can be. But that is not the kind of faith that I'm talking about here. This chapter is about the kind of faith necessary to reach your commitments. It's a Fundamental for anyone who wants to "stand their ground" and keep their commitments.

Does "faith" really matter in my life? Yes. Without a doubt, yes. And I intend to show you exactly why it matters so much.

Does "faith" always work? Well, if you're asking me whether faith means you magically get what you want all the time...then, no. Faith doesn't always work. Obviously, the other teams we played against thought that they could beat us, but lost anyway. So faith is not some magical, wish-granting genie in a bottle. The kind of faith I'm going to be talking about is much less exciting. But I assure you...it's absolutely vital.

So what was Chris Conwell (and the other seniors) really talking about? What is faith?

Well, let's start with what Real Faith isn't.

REAL FAITH ISN'T HOCUS-POCUS

See, a lot of people feel like faith is this mystical power that's impossible to grasp. It's a magic spell to get what you want. After all, we hear all the time that "if you believe it, you can achieve it." Right? So is faith really a magic spell?

No, it's not. Actually, faith is a very everyday, non-magical kind of thing. It's really, well, normal.

Don't believe me?

Think about this: you purchase a ticket to a football game, or a concert, or some event that will take place on a certain future date. You shell out your money *in faith* that this event will take place and you will be there to see it. That's faith, isn't it? If you didn't count on actually being there, then you wouldn't have put your money on it.

Or what about this simple test: you walk up to a chair. You sit on the chair. You place all your weight on it *in faith* that the chair will hold you up and not send you crashing to the ground. Isn't that also faith? Of course it takes a little more faith for some of us big guys than for others, but that's not my point. If you didn't think the chair could hold you, you wouldn't have sat on it in the first place. That's faith.

> If you didn't think the chair could hold you, you wouldn't have sat on it in the first place. That's faith.

Maybe you never even realized it, but we all use faith *every day!*

Honestly, if we didn't have faith, we'd never get out of bed in the morning because we wouldn't trust our feet to hold us up. Actually, we probably wouldn't even sleep in beds because we wouldn't trust that they could hold us up either. I mean, when you think about it, without faith, we wouldn't have friends or family (because people might let us down) or even things (because we can't trust them not to break). We'd pretty much live by ourselves outside somewhere, alone and destitute.

Doesn't sound very appealing, does it?

When you think about it, almost every single thing we do every day requires at least a little bit of faith. It isn't just a "church" thing. It isn't some magical, Harry Potter-type thing. It's real. And you use it every day.

REAL FAITH ISN'T REALLY BLIND

Let's say you asked a hundred people what faith is. What would they say?

Most people will probably tell you that faith is when you believe some delusional idea that doesn't have any basis in history or reality. They call it "blind" faith. And in their minds, it's not a good thing.

See, a lot of people think that faith is a cop-out. It's a crutch for someone who can't face reality square in the face. It's believing something because somebody told you to believe it. It's believing in things you can't back up or prove.

And these people think that anyone who would have faith is an idiot, a follower, someone who just can't survive in this world on their own two feet.

Don't worry...that kind of faith is NOT what I'm talking about here.

Now, don't get me wrong. There are people who believe in stuff without any good reason or evidence to back it up. They just "have faith" that it's true. *That* is blind faith. And it usually leads to getting scammed or being embarrassed. Definitely not a good thing!

It happens all the time. Blind faith plays out whenever you follow someone or something without worrying about where it might lead you. You let others think for you. You just assume they won't lead you wrong.

For example, say you ask a friend if she knows how to get to Friday night's away football game. She swears she does. She's driven to that school lots of times, she says, and she gives you detailed directions. So, instead of double-checking her with Google Maps or your GPS, you just start driving. And 45 minutes later, you realize that she sent you in the wrong direction!

That is blind faith. You should have checked out her directions to make sure they were right. But you didn't. And it got you lost in a city you'd never driven in before. Not fun.

Clearly, blind faith is just stupid.

But thankfully, I'm talking about Real Faith. And Real Faith is NOT "blind (stupid) faith."

Real Faith is based on personal knowledge. You're not just following along while someone else thinks for you. You don't believe something because someone told you it was true. You've checked it out. You've tried it out and found it to be true. Real Faith means putting your faith in something that has evidence of a good track record.

Like what happened at the end of one of the Indiana Jones movies, "The Last Crusade."

Picture this: Dr. Jones (Indiana Jones) is standing on the edge of a cliff that looks out over a huge ravine. There is treasure on the other side. His treasure map shows the only way across is to walk on thin air! That's impossible, right? But up to this point, his map has been true and has gotten him through many dangerous traps. So he decides to put faith in his map one last time. He understands the risk that he may fall to his untimely death. But he takes a leap of faith forward and...

To our surprise, his foot lands on solid ground! Instead of falling to his death, he is being held up by something unseen. When he leans to the side, he can see that the ravine is actually an illusion, and that the bridge across blended invisibly into the scenery when he was looking at it head on.

So what's the point?

The point is that Jones was showing Real Faith. If there was no map, or if the map had never been tested, then taking that "leap of faith" would have been blind faith. But because the map had already gotten him through two other tests, Jones knew he could trust it. And he made his "leap of faith" based on that fact. What looked impossible somehow also seemed probable because it was based on a track record of success.

> Blind faith won't get us anywhere because it isn't founded on anything at all.

That is what I'm talking about. Blind faith won't get us anywhere because it isn't founded on anything at all. But Real Faith is based on experience, knowledge, research. You know it's trustworthy because you've thought about it, tested it, and found it to be reliable.

And then, instead of being something foolish...Real Faith becomes something powerful.

So Real Faith isn't some mysterious thing from religion or fantasy movies, and it isn't some blind acceptance of what other people tell you.

But what IS it? Let me break it down for you.

WHAT FAITH IS.

Real Faith is what makes it possible for us to keep our commitments. Without it, we won't accomplish even the smallest step toward achieving our goals. Plain and simple: If you don't have faith, I guarantee you won't keep your commitment.

But most people don't realize that Real Faith has TWO parts. And that's why Real Faith is so rare. Lots of people have one part or the other, but not both, and then they wonder why their "faith" isn't working for them. Trust me...it doesn't work that way. If you don't have both, you don't have Real Faith.

So what are the two parts of Real Faith?

Part #1: Belief
This is the part of Real Faith that most people already know about.

Faith is a belief that something is true. Or is going to be true. Or can come true.

Real Faith has to start with how you THINK. It starts with a decision to believe in a person or an idea or a goal. It means looking at a situation and deciding that the outcome you want to happen CAN happen.

Now some of you are probably thinking, "Great, Joel! I totally believe in thinking positively. If I just believe something enough, it'll happen."

Sorry to disappoint you. That's not exactly what I'm talking about here.

Real Faith is more than just "positive thinking." It's a deeper belief. Think about Chris Conwell again. He (and the other seniors that year) started out with a belief that something was possible. They had decided that they could win a National Championship, no matter what the critics said. Their faith was totally grounded in that way of thinking.

The same is true for everyone who makes a commitment. How you think (and what you think) is absolutely critical to everything you do. What you believe will make a difference in how you live.

Think about the movie *The Matrix*. For the entire movie, Morpheus is convinced that Neo is the One. But no one else, including Neo, sees it. As they fight the Agents, nothing seems to indicate that Neo has the powers the One is supposed to have. Then suddenly, at the climax of the movie, both Trinity and Neo begin to believe in him. They realize he is the One, and he single-handedly defeats the Agents and saves his friends.

What changed for Neo in the movie? His circumstances hadn't changed. But his faith in himself did. And when he began to think differently, he was able to accomplish more than he thought was possible.

> If you can't see yourself accomplish your goal, it is not likely you'll ever achieve it.

The same will always be true for you, too. If you can't see yourself accomplish your goal, it is not likely you'll ever achieve it.

But just believing in yourself or in someone else or in a commitment you have made is not enough. Real Faith has a second, even more important, ingredient.

Part #2: Action

See, faith is based on belief, but BELIEF IS NOT FAITH.

Or maybe I should say that belief *alone* is not faith.

HUH?

I know, it's kinda confusing. But stay with me for a minute.

Think about it, don't most people use the words *faith* and *belief* interchangeably? Well, they are similar, but there is a big difference.

Belief doesn't really make you go anywhere or do anything; it's simply your own conviction. Real Faith, on the other hand, is all about *action*. In *The Matrix*, Morpheus believed in Neo for the entire movie. But his belief was not enough. It wasn't until Neo believed, and *acted on that belief,* that amazing things started to happen.

Belief alone didn't make Neo "the One." He had to do something with that belief - he had to ACT on it.

The same is true for you.

You can *believe* that the concert will take place, but if you don't actually buy a ticket, is that really *faith*? No. You can *believe* that the chair won't collapse when you sit on it, but if you don't actually try it, then is that really *faith*? Nope. And of course, if Indiana Jones only *believed* he would make it across the ravine without actually taking a step out onto nothing, it would have been a really anticlimactic movie. He had to have real *faith*. He had to take a step.

The *action* step is why Coach Tressel makes Real Faith one of his Fundamentals. Just believing is not enough. But when you add action to your belief, amazing things will begin to happen.

BUT FAITH IN WHAT?

Now some of you may be wondering, "How do I know what to put my faith in? Are you talking about faith in God or some higher being? What happens if I put my faith in something I thought was dependable, but it ends up letting me down?"

Good question.

Let's go back to our examples: buying tickets, sitting in a chair, stepping out onto a bridge. When you buy tickets to that game or concert, who are you putting your faith in? When you sit in a chair, what are you putting your faith in? When Indiana Jones stepped out onto that bridge, what was he putting his faith in?

Okay, sorry for the pop quiz.

But think about it. To buy tickets to a concert, you have faith *in the band and the concert organizers* to do their jobs. To sit in a chair, you put your faith *in that chair* to hold you up. Jones put his faith in his map to get him through one more test. Sure, these are pretty basic examples, but the point is simple.

You have to put your faith in the person or object that you need to get you to your goal. You want to see the concert? You have to trust the band. You want to sit down? You have to trust the chair. That is how Real Faith always works.

But here's where things get interesting. See, in every example I've been using, you're putting your faith into something (or someone) that YOU HAVE NO CONTROL OVER.

You don't have any say about whether the football game gets rained out, or the concert gets cancelled, or the chair has a weak leg, or there's an invisible bridge, but you still put your faith in them enough to take action which may be irreversible. You could be out money if the concert is cancelled. You might break your tailbone if the chair gives way. Indiana Jones might just as easily have fallen to his death.

Every day you put your faith in things you can't control. But wouldn't it be easier, or even better, to put faith in something you CAN control?

"Like what, Joel?"

How about YOU?

You can't control your friends, your circumstances, the bolts in every chair you sit down on, or the weather the day of the concert you've been dying to see.

But...

> But wouldn't it be easier, or even better, to put faith in something you CAN control?

You CAN control yourself, your attitudes, your decisions. You DO have control over how you will react in a stressful situation. You DO have control over how you will handle adversity. You DO have control over whether you're going to give into temptation. You DO have the ability to make commitments and keep pursuing them, no matter what.

Maybe it's time to start putting your faith in what you can control – You!

BELIEVING IS SEEING

Of course, I know that's not as easy as it might sound, right? But it's still true.

If you want to reach your goals, you have to believe in yourself, the one person you can control. It's called having self-confidence.

Of course, most of us have some self-confidence. Most of us know we aren't entirely worthless. But still, when it comes to making a commitment and pursing Significance, the very last person we're ready to put our faith in is ourselves, isn't it?

Think about it. If your brother wants to make the baseball team, you are ready to encourage him. If your best friend is working to finish the final level of *Sniper: Ghost Warrior* on XBox, you have his back. If your girlfriend is hoping to get promoted at work, you tell her how much she deserves it.

But when the goal is yours, when the commitment depends on you, suddenly, that confidence starts to waiver. You aren't as sure that you have what it takes to achieve your dreams. You believe in other people, but totally bail when it comes to believing in your own talents, abilities, goals and commitments.

So what do we do? We have to practice Real Faith...in ourselves.

Wait...did you just say *practice* Faith? Yep...I did. Believe it or not, Real Faith takes practice. You have to cultivate it, nurture it, feed it, make it grow.

And there are a couple of good ways you can do this.

First, remember how we talked about breaking your commitment into smaller goals? Well, having Real Faith means that you believe in yourself enough to tackle the first small goal. And only that goal. Focus on that step until it's done. Then, when it's accomplished, you have proof that putting Faith in yourself was a good idea. So your confidence grows. And you start to think maybe you can handle the next step, too. And the next step. And the next.

As you achieve each new goal, you gain more confidence to tackle the next goal. It becomes a positive cycle of Thinking + Action (or Real Faith) that will, before you know it, help you see your commitment become a reality.

And there is a second good way to practice Real Faith. It's called "visualization."

I know, it sounds like a psychology experiment, or like a bunch of people sitting around, holding their fingers to their temples and humming. Okay, that actually would be weird. So I wouldn't recommend trying this in a group…maybe you can work on it while you're daydreaming in English class instead.

Here's what it might look like:

Take a few minutes and reflect on a commitment that you want to make. Even better, go back to the commitment you wrote down at the end of the last chapter.

Okay…with that commitment in mind, ask yourself, "Do I believe it?" No really, do you really believe it? Close your eyes. Think of your commitment again.

1. *Create a scenario where it might be tough to stand your ground.* See in your mind the obstacles that might come up. See all the things that might distract you from your goal: boyfriends or girlfriends, a job, laziness, video games…you know, things like that.

2. *Picture yourself staying strong again, even when others stop believing.* Picture the people who might try to stop you or slow you down. Maybe a family member. Maybe a coach or even someone in your neighborhood. Then picture yourself ignoring their comments and criticism. See yourself continuing to move forward.

3. *Envision yourself keeping that commitment.* See yourself putting in long hours of work. See yourself turning down some activities you really wanted to do. See yourself making progress. Then, finally, see yourself reaching that goal, keeping your commitment. See it really come true. Envision the moment that you buy that car, get that diploma, make the team.

Great. That is visualization.

But once is not enough. Do it every day, until it becomes second nature. Regularly take the time to ask yourself, "Do I really believe that I can keep this commitment? Do I really have what it takes?" If you can answer yes to both of those questions, you are good to go. You can step out and start moving forward.

You might be thinking, "Eh, okay Joel, that's good for some people, but I don't think I need all that positive thinking mental stuff."

Really? Well, let me paint a picture for you...

Coach Heacock, the Defensive Line Coach at Ohio State, often told us about a study where one group of people practiced shooting free throws for several hours

> But once is not enough. Do it every day, until it becomes second nature.

and another group just visualized themselves making free throws. Then the two groups competed to see who made the most free throws. Do you know who won? The team that had visualized without ever touching a basketball.

Crazy, huh? Maybe this "visualizing" stuff is worth a try after all. For free throws *and* for commitments.

CRAZY OR CONFIDENT?

Real Faith is the foundation for reaching your commitments. Faith is so powerful that it doesn't matter what comes your way. Your faith can be unwavering. Are your best friends making fun of you? Doesn't matter, you will keep your commitment. Feeling kind of down this week? Again, not a problem. You will hold onto your commitment because of your Faith.

Of course, some people might call that "crazy" and not "faith." That's what I thought about Chris Conwell as a freshman during training camp. But he wasn't crazy. He was just really confident. He knew that we could win. He had Real Faith.

Of course there was no guarantee that we would win the National Championship. But as much as it depended on him as one of our senior leaders, Chris had confidence in his own work ethic, effort, and abilities, and he knew he would be able to do his part. He had Faith in himself.

The funny thing was, he didn't start out that way. He was once a lowly freshman like me! But he practiced Real Faith. It took time, belief in himself, and commitment in order to win one little victory after another along the way. Over time he grew in Faith until his senior year, when he had seen enough evidence to know that together he and his teammates could overcome any obstacle.

> But he wasn't crazy. He was just really confident.

And he was right.

That year, Faith was our most important Fundamental. Our belief was based on evidence of success, one little victory at a time. We put our belief into action. The reward was a National Championship.

What will your reward be? It all starts with Real Faith.

MAKING IT PERSONAL

1. Joel talks about faith as an 'everyday' thing. Do you agree or disagree with him? Is faith really 'normal,' or do you still think of it as a 'hocus-pocus' kind of thing? Can you think of examples, other than the ones in the chapter, in which we use faith in daily life?

_____

_____

_____

2. What do you think about when you hear the expression "blind faith"? Do you agree with Joel that 'blind faith' means believing in something without evidence or reason? What are some reasons why people might still have 'blind faith'?

_____

_____

_____

3. Joel says that faith is a combination of 1) Belief and 2) Action. Do you think both parts are really necessary? Which part is harder for you: to believe or to act on your beliefs?

_____

_____

_____

4.   Do you think that it is really necessary to have faith in YOURSELF to keep your commitments? Will a lack of self-confidence keep someone from his or her goals? Why or why not?

_____

_____

_____

5.   When Joel talked about visualization, what ideas came into your mind? Do you think that visualization is a good tool to build your faith? Try using visualization with the commitment you made in Chapter 4. What did your visualization look like?

_____

_____

_____

6.   In his story, Joel describes the first time that Chris Conwell said he believed OSU would win the Championship. If you had been in Joel's place, would Chris have seemed crazy or confident to you? By the end of the story, do you think your opinion would have changed? Why or why not?

_____

_____

_____

CHAPTER 6:
FIGHT
"Joel and the Hot Gymnast"

Warning: This may get awkward.

What you are about to read has to do with sex. Yes, I said it, S-E-X.

Don't freak out! It won't be as bad as you think. Just avoid reading this chapter out loud in a public place...

I guess the first thing I should say is that sex is something that guys think about a lot.

"Um...duh. No kidding, Joel, thanks for sharing. I knew that part."

Of course, everyone knows that part. But stick with me for a second. See, I think a lot of guys try really hard to pretend they don't think about sex that much. And I suspect most girls don't have a clue just how obsessed with sex guys can be.

Just avoid reading this chapter out loud in a public place...

Think of it like this...You know how some songs get stuck in your head? Something with a catchy beat or cool lyric that your mind just keeps playing over and over. You aren't even thinking about the song, but all of a sudden, you find yourself singing it.

You even try to listen to other music to get it out of there, but an hour later, it's still there.

For teenage guys, sex is that song that gets stuck in your head. It's there ALL. THE. TIME. From age 12 on. And there is absolutely nothing guys can do to change the station. I mean, sure, there are times when they are thinking about other things, but before long, all guys find themselves hearing that same old "Sex Song" again.

Now you may be wondering, "Um, Joel...I thought this chapter was about Fighting for our commitments. What does sex have to do with anything?

Well, in my case, it has a lot to do with commitments.

See, I've talked a lot about my football commitment and what it took to see that dream become a reality. But that's not the only commitment I ever made. When I was in junior high, I made a second commitment. A more personal one.

I decided that I wasn't going to have sex until I was married.

I know, I know. That might sound strange. And I'm sure someone just rolled their eyes and wondered, "But why, Joel? What's wrong with sex?"

And my answer...absolutely nothing.

I'm not opposed to sex. I just decided that I wanted to wait for it until I was married. And I had a few good reasons for making that commitment.

At first, it just seemed like the right thing to do. My parents and others taught me that having sex before marriage was wrong. I believed them. I still do. But I'll be honest. The older I got, the more I began to wonder if I would have the will power to do what I thought was right. The "Sex Song" was getting louder.

Then came Eighth Grade Health class with Mrs. Stevenson. And Sex Ed. Oh, Sex Ed. My friends and I struggled not to laugh when someone said something that even resembled something sexual. How would we ever survive *a teacher* talking about it for an entire quarter?

But we did survive. We survived the two-week ordeal of "parenting" an electronic baby that would keep track of whether we dropped it or let it cry too long. It was supposed to scare us about the responsibilities and reality of teen pregnancy. Frankly, it did. I hated waking up in the middle of the night to rock that dumb doll.

But the really scary stuff was next...we had to learn about Sexually Transmitted Diseases. Mrs. Stevenson showed us detailed charts and graphs about how many people (even our age) were getting these diseases. The numbers were crazy! But even worse, she showed us disgusting videos and pictures of people who were infected. Was she allowed to do this to us? Walking into fourth period health class was like going to see a horror movie every day.

After that, I had a second motivation to keep my commitment to avoid sex before marriage: No STD's! I wanted nothing to do with the permanent, life-changing effects of having an STD.

But then, Sex Ed ended. And so did the fear. Within a couple weeks, the pictures that scarred our minds were forgotten. Within a few months, the dangers of sex weren't so serious. We had long forgotten about how challenging it was to take care of a plastic baby for 2 weeks.

But I still felt like the "Sex Song" was always pounding in my head. How was I really going to be able to keep my commitment?

Fortunately, my parents had taught me to step back every once in a while and think about the future. I started to think about not just the type of girl I wanted to date, but the type of woman I wanted to marry. And I made a mental "checklist" of all the traits and qualities I wanted my wife to have.

It was my Future Wife Wish List. You know, things like honesty, intelligence, sense of humor, and of course, good looking.

Oh, and one thing was certain: I really wanted her to be a virgin. For some reason I really wanted complete physical intimacy to be something that she would share *only* with me. It made me kind of sick to think otherwise. I mean, I would deal with it if she wasn't a virgin. But man, in my mind, how great would it be if we both set aside this part of our lives for when we were married.

Then common sense kicked in. As much as I wanted my future wife to have sex only with me, why would she be okay with *me* having sex with a bunch of different girls? This idea became my new primary motivation for my commitment. I even told my parents and my friends that I was committed to abstinence.

I thought I had it all figured out because I had three solid reasons for my commitment to save sex for marriage.

- It was wrong.
- It was dangerous.
- It could hurt my future wife.

And that, ladies and gentlemen, is when the fight really began.

See, I didn't recognize that just having a few reasons was not enough. I could have a million of the best reasons in the world, but that wouldn't

> I didn't recognize that just having a few reasons was not enough.

keep me from breaking my commitment. The "Sex Song" was too loud. And I wasn't prepared to fight for it.

Truth is, in high school, I said, "I'm saving sex for marriage." But my actions told a different story.

Whenever I was alone with my girlfriend, my desires took over, and my commitment flew out the window. I inched closer and closer to breaking my commitment. I barely tried to fight at all. Truthfully, if it hadn't been for the self-control of some of the girls I dated, my commitment would have died in high school.

So what was wrong? I knew I could keep a commitment. After all, look what I'd achieved on the football field. But in the arena of sex, it seemed all bets were off. Thankfully, the flaw in my plan to fight the "Sex Song" wasn't really all that hard to see. Truth was, there was absolutely no way my high school strategy was going to work.

See, I began several relationships with the best intentions, but when the "Sex Song" would begin to play very loudly in my head, we would get as close to sex as possible. I guess I thought that if I got as close to the line as I could without stepping over it, I was still succeeding.

Really?! *That* was my plan?

I felt like such an idiot. Had I really tried to fight for my commitment with such a bad plan? Yep. And to make matters worse, I realized just how badly I'd treated the girls I dated. When things got too close to the line, I did what every mature young man would do: I would break up with her. Out of the blue. Nice, huh? Yep, looking back, I realized that I was just hurting the people I cared about, confusing myself, and not really fighting for my commitment.

So, before I went to Ohio State, I took a long, hard look at my life. I knew I was staring failure in the face unless something changed. So I changed my strategy.

I decided to put real effort into fighting for my commitment. And I made a new plan. No more "get as close to the line as possible." I had to stay as far away from the line as possible so that I would not be as tempted.

I renewed my commitment. And *this time,* I was ready to fight for it.

And then came Bethany.

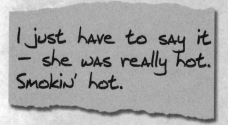

She led meetings for "Athletes in Action," a group I joined my fresh-man year at Ohio State. About 40 athletes from various OSU teams met on Wednesday evenings. I made some great friends there. But it was Bethany who always caught my eye. I just have to say it — she was really hot. Smokin' hot. But, she was a pop-ular junior on the gymnastics team, and I was a freshman. She was *completely* out of my league. I knew she'd never date me, but I still hoped that we could perhaps be friends.

Thankfully, that part worked out pretty well for me. Through the weekly Athletes in Action meetings, Bethany and I did be-come friends. We often stayed after the meetings to talk with a few other people. Sometimes she even gave me a ride back to my dorm since she had a car and I didn't.

Then, one night as I was doing homework in my dorm room (yes, I actually did homework), Bethany showed up at the door. Maybe she'd come to profess her love for me!

Or not. Really she had come to give me a gymnastics team poster that she and her teammates were hanging up in the dorms. But I still thought it was great. She had stopped by to give me a poster personally! And smack dab in the middle of the large team photo was her beautiful face. I hung the poster on my dorm room wall so that every morning I woke up to see the girl of my dreams.

Obviously, my plan to "just be friends" was failing miserably. No matter how hard I tried to pretend otherwise, I really wanted to date her. I even started to consider what a future with her would be like. Of course, I was pretty sure she wasn't a virgin. I didn't know anyone that popular and attractive who hadn't had sex. But I decided that I would be willing to sacrifice my dream of marrying a virgin for someone like her. She was just too good to be true.

We continued to talk and spend a lot of time together. I started to think I might have a shot with her, but I had no idea where she stood. Thankfully, she didn't leave me wondering for long. One day as we were about to leave my dorm room, she stopped me. "No. We need to talk first."

"So..." she said and looked down at her hands. We were sitting on separate chairs facing my desk and computer. We both still had our jackets on, ready to go.

"Where is this going?" She asked without looking at me.

Suddenly I got nervous; I didn't respond.

"Are we dating?" I could tell it was extremely difficult for her to ask. But instantly all of my anxiety was gone. She wanted to be with me!

"Yes! I mean, I would love to...do you feel the same way?" It came out a little awkward, but I didn't care. I was too excited.

"Of course!" she replied with a huge smile on her face. Then we hugged for a *long* time. I couldn't believe how lucky I was.

But the "Sex Song" was the loudest it had ever been. And the real fight for my "No-Sex" commitment was just beginning. I knew that we needed to talk, *soon*. But I was nervous. Do people talk about those things? Is it too weird? Would she laugh at me? Did she even share any type of similar commitment? I had no idea where she stood.

But the next time we went out to eat together, I decided to man up. And finally, the topic came up. I was totally honest with her. I told her all about my history with girls and about my commitment to abstinence. As hard as it was, I even admitted my failures in the past and my re-commitment before college. I wanted to set up some serious guidelines as we started to date. And I told her that, hard as it would be, I thought it would be worth it in the long run. Finally, I let her speak.

And I was totally shocked by her response.

Turned out that she was actually a virgin, too! And had recently made the exact same commitment as me. I was so relieved. And excited. I had found someone who actually wanted to fight for the decision to wait until marriage. She really was the perfect girl!

So that night we made our battle plan.

1. *Curfew.* We knew that the later it got at night, the weaker our self-control became. Coach Tressel always said, "Nothing good happens after 10 p.m." I was starting to see what he meant.
2. *Emotional boundaries.* We made certain topics of conversation off-limits. Marriage? It could wait. Kids? No way. These things would only create an emotional intimacy that would tempt us to become intimate physically.
3. *Physical boundaries.* No games of "how close can we get." Instead we made sure we couldn't even see the line. Our rule: stay far away from anything that resembled sexual intimacy. Hot tub in a bathing suit? Bad idea. Lying down and 'talking?' Not a chance. My parents always told me that lying

down with a girl was not a good idea. Now I understood what they meant.

That night was the first time I actually felt confident about my commitment to abstinence. I finally felt prepared for the challenges ahead, and I had someone that was willing to fight alongside me. I knew our battle plan was a tough one, but we were committed to hold one another to the strategy and fight for it.

And you know what?

I had no idea just how hard it would actually be. Fighting for this commitment was, in some ways, way harder than working to be a good football player. There were some really rough nights. Frustration. Tears. That "Sex Song" in my head never quit. The battle was long, and there was constant temptation to give up and give in. And that was before we got engaged. Once I proposed, the fight got even tougher.

> That night was the first time I actually felt confident about my commitment to abstinence.

But, we fought our way through.

And because of the fight, we learned some really important stuff. That our relationship was not based on physical chemistry. That our decision to get married wasn't clouded by physical needs and desires. That we were a good team, and together, we could achieve just about anything we set our minds to.

As cheesy as it sounds, it really was all worth it the day we shared our first kiss. Family and friends from all over the country came to watch. In fact, we invited them to watch. See, we had our first kiss just after we were presented as husband and wife. Yes, you heard me. We had our first kiss on our wedding day. It was awesome! Yep, that day it was all worth it. And I'll tell you the truth, that night it was all worth it too! (Ok, you can puke now.)

YOU GOTTA FIGHT

"LADIES AND GENTLEMEN...Welcome to tonight's MAIN EVENT. The bout will be a 3-round, winner-take-all battle for the fate of your commitment! Contenders...are you ready?"

Well, are you? Are you really ready to fight for your commitments? No more excuses. No tapping out. Are you ready to get into the ring and see what you're made of?

I wasn't. I thought I was. I thought I was fighting and winning my battle to save sex for marriage. But in high school, I was failing miserably. I don't want you to find yourself in the same place with the commitment you have made.

So what does this look like? How does fighting for your commitments actually work?

ROUND 1: *Expect the Fight.*
DING!

In a boxing match, the bell sounds, and the two boxers circle each other in the ring, right? But if that's all they do for the entire three minutes, it won't be a very exciting match. One of the most important things that happens in the first round is that someone throws the first punch. I mean, nobody gets into a boxing ring without expecting to get punched. It's assumed. It's a given.

Now, we all know that life is a battle; it's a fight. A lot of people struggle with a lot of really bad stuff. People face problems at home, at school, at work. They might get a serious illness. Or run out of money. Or wonder why everyone in life lets them down.

I hear a lot about this kind of stuff from the students I meet while speaking. Often they sound like Jenna:

Dear Joel,

No other kid has had the same situation I have had and I pray to God that no one else does. No one else deserves to go through what I am going through now. I know that life isn't always fair but there is no reason that I should be going through this. The pain and hurt of what happened still gets to me and I can't let it go; it hurts so bad. I never expected this road block to come. I'm surprised I haven't just broken down. I am so sad and I have to fake being someone I'm really not. I have lost who I used to be. I don't even know who I am anymore....... -Jenna

Sounds tough, doesn't it? Obviously, what Jenna is going through sucks. And the truth is, everyone has times when they feel just like her. We feel like we've been punched. Hard.

So yeah, life itself is a battle. I get that. But what I'm talking about here goes beyond the reality that "life sucks."

As soon as you sign up for a commitment, you are signing up to compete in a serious fight. You are guaranteed to be challenged. You just moved from the Featherweight division to the Heavyweight division. And it isn't going to be easy.

Oh, we think it is. A lot of people make commitments just thinking of how cool it would be to say that we set a goal and accomplished it. We don't think about the road we have set out on and where it might take us. We definitely don't think about the fact that the road might get tough and take huge unexpected turns.

In boxing terms...a lot of people like to imagine how cool their name will sound when the announcer's voice booms it out over the crowd. They imagine pretty girls carrying signs between rounds. They imagine standing at the center of the ring after Round 3 while the referee holds up their hand as the victor.

But they forget that between each of those moments are a lot of punches. And bruises. And pain. They forget about the actual FIGHT.

> They forget that between each of those moments are a lot of punches. And bruises. And pain.

This even happened at Ohio State. Some football players wanted to just show up and bask in the glory of Ohio State Football stardom. They did not expect it to be such a challenge physically, mentally, and emotionally. It was hard enough to handle school and football, let alone anything else. Even though being on the Ohio State football team was one of the most desirable positions in the country, every year, a good handful of athletes quit.

Why? Because they weren't expecting the fight. I don't want you to ignore the battle. Expect to have to fight for your commitments.

But who are you fighting? What are you up against? Well, there are two possible opponents.

First, there's you. Yep. That's right. You may end up being one of your own greatest opponents.

Huh?

Well, just think about it. You have made a big commitment. It's going to be challenging. It should be challenging. You're pushing yourself further than you've ever gone before. But that means, at some point, you will be tempted to give up. There will be times when it won't seem worth it. You'll be tired, worn down, just plain beat. And you, the person who desires to make a change, will want to break your commitment.

I did.

There were lots of times when I was ready to just give up on my commitments. A lot of other guys quit lifting weights in the off-season. But I didn't. And some days it was hard to make myself go to the weight room by myself. Or when my friends started drinking. There were some nights when I really wanted to give up and join them. After all, missing one workout wasn't going to tank my commitment, was it? And one beer wouldn't really have been that bad, right?

Wrong, of course. I knew those thoughts would only get me in trouble. But some days, I really wanted to give up my commitment and go along with the crowd. So yeah, trust me, sometimes you will be your own opponent.

Other times, your opponents will come from the outside.

Like other people. Or your circumstances. Or sometimes, it's our culture. See, we tend to think it's bad to experience tough times, so when things get hard, we just try to escape. We want to change schools, jobs, girlfriends, or sports teams as soon as something happens that we don't like.

But no matter who your opponent is, if you expect the fight, you'll be better prepared to deal with it.

That was another lesson I learned the hard way. In high school, I didn't know that my commitment to football would cost me my friends. That was a sacrifice I hadn't anticipated. And it was a battle I didn't fight well.

Would I have preferred to keep my friends while I achieved my goal of becoming the best football player I could be? Of course. But I didn't see any other option at the time. I chose one over the other. But if I'd thought ahead a little bit, maybe I could have kept my commitment without losing every friend I had.

Lesson learned. And when it came to my commitment to save sex for marriage, I thought ahead.

I knew some people would disagree with me. And I promise you, they did. I felt the pressure from people around me. I mean, I had committed not to have sex until I was married. That's not a common way of doing things. Some people totally agreed with me, but most people thought I was out of my mind. It was a battle, but this time I was ready.

And who was right? Well, I kept that commitment. And I can assure you that having to fight for it only made the success that much sweeter.

ROUND 2: *Execute the Game Plan*

Imagine yourself on a sunny Saturday afternoon in October. Ohio State is playing at The Shoe, and the game is about to start. Now picture yourself, not in the stands, but on the field. It's your big moment. You are actually playing in a game for the Ohio State Buckeyes. You run out onto the field with your teammates and wait for the game to start.

How do you feel? I can tell you from experience that you'll feel overwhelmed. Your stomach is in knots. The pressure is intense. You don't want to screw up. How do you keep your nerves from destroying your chances to play well?

Stick to the fundamentals. Execute the game plan.

If you want to win the game, you have to have a plan and put it into action. And if you want to keep your commitments, the same rules apply. Now, we already talked about creating a plan for keeping your commitment. You have to know the goal and break it down into smaller goals.

But what happens when things don't happen just like you thought they would? What happens when you find yourself in the middle of a fight for your commitments and the pressure is on?

You stick to the fundamentals. You execute your game plan.

I knew that keeping my commitment to save sex for marriage was not going to be easy. And it wasn't. But when the battle got really intense, Bethany and I had already decided what we were going to do.

Remember our battle plan: curfew, emotional boundaries, physical boundaries. Because we had that plan in place, we didn't have to worry about knowing what we "should" do. If it was approaching our curfew, we said good night. We didn't spend time in hot tubs. And if our conversation got too close to an "off-limits" topic, we changed the subject.

The battle lines had been drawn long before any of the tough times came. And because we already had our plan in place, we were ready when the fight began. It was just a matter of doing those things. And doing them again. And again. Until we had accomplished our goal.

You have a game plan in place. You know the fundamentals. When the pressure is on, simply execute your plan. That's how you win the battle.

You have a game plan in place. You know the fundamentals. When the pressure is on, simply execute your plan.

ROUND 3: *Attitude Gets the Knockout*

You want to win the fight for your commitment? You expect to fight. You have a game plan. Good. Now, there is one more thing you need.

The most important thing. Your greatest weapon is your attitude.

Look, life is hard. We've discussed that. And the fight only gets harder when you make a commitment. I've mentioned that, too. But when will things change? When does the tide turn in your favor?

Sometimes, not for a long time. Remember Jenna? She wrote me again a few months later...

Dear Joel,

Things with my situation haven't gotten any better. I just can't take it anymore. I really did think things were just starting to get better but then something else happens and I don't know what to do anymore. I just want to give up. I really hope this all comes to an end but I just can't see the light at the end of this tunnel... –Jenna

I felt just like Jenna more than once in the fight for my commitment. I made my decision, but didn't do so hot in high school. Okay, no problem. I recommitted before college. Surely it would be easier at this stage because I was ready to fight now. Nope...meeting Bethany made it harder, not easier. And after we got engaged, did the battle lessen? Nope again. Every stage got a little harder.

It was like climbing the first hill of a roller coaster. Was I ever going to make it to the top when the easy part happens? I sure didn't feel like it.

And that was when my attitude became really important.

We know we can't change our circumstances. And we can't change other people. We can't change the weather outside or the menu at the cafeteria today or that our best friend yelled at us last night. We have no control over any of those things.

But we can control our attitude. And that is why the right attitude makes all the difference in your fight.

In Coach Tressel's book, "The Winner's Manual," he explains it like this:

"Adversity comes to us all—it's only a matter of when. The real question is not whether we'll face adversity but how we will respond to it when it comes. If our attitude is one that embraces learning and growing, we'll treat adversity as a stepping-stone to the success we desire, rather than see it as an insurmountable obstacle. But if we have a negative attitude and become defensive at the first hint of criticism or begin to blame others for our mistakes, we'll miss the opportunity to develop into the types of people we want to be."

You want to fight to win? Change your attitude.

Coach Tressel is right. We should see adversity as an opportunity. A chance to grow, mature, find out who we are, and change for the better. We can actually use it to move ourselves closer to our goal.

You wouldn't step into a boxing ring without gloves would you? Of course not. Well, in the arena of commitments, having the right attitude is like putting your gloves on.

If we shift our attitude from "Oh poor me, this stuff sucks" to "This stuff sucks, but I can use it to grow if I just keep going," we will find ourselves able to stick it out when our opponent seems to be beating us badly. We can stay in the fight. We can stay and fight. And it's all about our attitude.

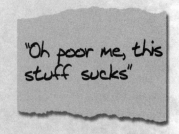

"Oh poor me, this stuff sucks"

That's what happened to Tyler.

In high school, Tyler played basketball. He wanted a scholarship to college, so he committed himself to get and keep a 3.5 GPA. And he was succeeding.

Then disaster struck. Tyler walked in on his best friend just after the friend had committed suicide. Obviously, this hit him really hard. He started drinking and not caring about much. His grades started to slip. And who could blame him? What was his commitment in the face of his friend's death?

But one teacher saw it differently. He could tell Tyler wasn't heading in the right direction. And he really understood. This teacher had experienced the same crisis, except that it was a sibling that he had witnessed take his own life.

So one day after school, he stopped Tyler in the hallway.

"You know, Ty, there are two ways you can handle what you are going though. First, you can keep going down the same path that you are on. You can drink away your problems and fill your life with self-pity and apathy. No one will blame you. You have experienced a horrible tragedy. Everyone feels sorry for you. Your second option is more difficult. You can decide to make the best of what has happened and learn from it. Grow from it. Be the person that people look at and think, 'Wow, I am really proud of him for rising above this tragedy. Not only has he risen above it, but he has become a better person because of it.' Tyler, it's your choice what option you choose. I challenge you to make the best decision."

That is exactly the attitude change I'm challenging you to make. Put on your gloves and get in the ring. Stop whining that you can't control the fight. Start seeing the fight as a chance to get closer to your goal. Make the choice. Throw your first punch.

You will have to fight for your commitments. But you can win that fight. Expect the hard times. Execute your game plan. And be sure you have a winner's attitude. Get in there and fight.

Oh, and one final note about Jenna. She won her battle, too... when she changed her attitude. I got this last email from her:

Dear Joel,

Things with my situation have gotten a lot better and I am actually excited for school to start. I've learned that life isn't perfect and what happened to me still hurts me a great deal but good things do come along and you have to take full advantage of them. I know there are still things that I can work on and I am going to try as hard as I can to make myself the best that I can be. You have helped me out in more ways than you could ever understand and I am so thankful for it. I hope one day I can do what you do and share my stories with kids and tell them that no matter what happens in life, you hold all the power to make it better or make it worse. It's all in how you handle it. It's up to you to choose what you do with your life and I have chosen to make mine the best that it can possibly be. When I think my life is at the worst point I am going to try even harder to make it better. I am going to see the light at the end of the tunnel. –Jenna

Yep...sounds like a victor's speech to me!

MAKING IT PERSONAL

1. What did you think of the email messages from Jenna in this chapter? Could you relate to some of the things she said about the difficulties she was facing? In what ways?

_____

_____

_____

2. Joel says that everyone should 'expect a fight' when it comes to keeping a commitment. Do you agree or disagree? Can keeping a commitment ever be easy?

_____

_____

_____

3. Think about the commitment you wrote down at the end of Chapter 4. What types of difficulties do you think you can you expect to encounter with your commitment? Which one would be the hardest for you to deal with?

_____

_____

_____

4. When you encounter difficulties in keeping your commitments, Joel says you need to just 'execute your game plan.' Do you think sticking to a plan will help you deal with adversity? Why or why not?

_____

_____

_____

5. Your attitude is the best weapon you have in your fight to keep your commitment. Can you think of an example where a bad attitude kept someone from doing what he or she wanted to do? Have you ever been in a situation where having a good attitude helped you?

_____

_____

_____

6. List some practical things that you can do to keep a positive attitude even when you are in a tough fight for your commitment.

_____

_____

_____

CHAPTER 7:

FRIENDS

"I Am Only One"

"Penton, get in there!"

I heard my name shouted by Coach Heacock, our Defensive Line Coach. I quickly turned and grabbed my helmet which was luckily sitting on the bench behind me. I threw it on my head, snapped the chinstrap, and pushed my way through the guys and onto the field. The grass felt softer than I remembered.

Just moments earlier I'd been standing on the sideline, day-dreaming about the next time I could take a nap and what restaurant my parents were going to take me to after the game. I wasn't paying much attention to what was happening on the field. Then, suddenly, I was in the game.

"I can't believe this is actually happening," I thought to myself.

It was the second game of the season, and we were playing at home against San Diego State. It was my first year of eligibility, and I was playing backup Defensive End behind Simon Frasier. We had won our first game fairly easily, so I was sent in with the rest of the second team to mop things up in the fourth quarter. The San Diego State game was supposed to be a blowout, so I expected that I might get into the game late in the 3rd quarter or so. You can imagine my shock when I heard my coach's booming voice call me into the game only a few minutes after kickoff – when we weren't even winning!

I joined the huddle and listened to the play call from our captain. My teammates didn't look at me or give my arrival a moment's thought. I lined up in my stance and got ready. When the ball was snapped, I lunged forward as fast and hard as I could. A few plays later, I left the field with the rest of the defense. My first first-quarter series was over.

To be honest, I didn't do that great of a job in that first appearance. I just tried to do what I had been taught and fulfill my responsibility. Each of us had a role that day; my role was Simon Frasier's backup. I was prepared to step up, and my teammates trusted me. Our roles might not have been glamorous, but each role, including mine, was important. We depended on each other to execute our roles. So that's what we did.

And that's what it means to be a team.

WE ALL NEED A TEAM

One of the reasons I love the game of football is that it teaches you how to be part of a team.

At Ohio State we leaned on each other, we depended on each other. We actually were so close that we called ourselves a "family." Now, I'll be honest...when I first heard the guys on my team use the term "Ohio State Football Family," I kind of laughed it off. Were they serious? It didn't take long to see they all bought into this concept. When we said we were a family, we meant it.

Coaches and players were not only constantly together, but we also looked out for each other. We cared about each other. I quickly came to understand that my teammates would always have my back. And they knew that I would always have theirs.

And guess what? *You* need a team, too. Now, I could spend a lot of time talking about your family or the Boy Scouts here, but

I'm not going to. I'm going to talk about one really important team...maybe the most important team you have.

Your friends.

"Wow, Joel...my friends? A team? Really? Have you met my friends? Um, 'cause they aren't exactly the same things as the Buckeyes, you know..."

Doesn't matter. These are the people I'm going to talk about in this chapter. Think for a minute about your friends. You know...the people you hang out with. The guys you eat lunch with. The girls you go shopping with. Those friends...the really good ones.

Got them in mind? Good. Now, listen to this...

Your friends are going to have a serious influence on your ability to make and keep your commitments.

Did you hear me? It doesn't matter what the commitment is, your friends are the primary "team" that will influence whether or not you reach that goal. Scary thought, huh? Well, it shouldn't be. Or at least, it doesn't have to be. If you have really good friends, you are well on your way to having the support you're going to need to reach your goal.

> It doesn't matter what the commitment is, your friends are the primary "team" that will influence whether or not you reach that goal.

Just think about what a good team of friends can do...

THEY HELP US DO MORE THAN WE CAN DO ALONE

Okay...let's get one thing straight right here: you can't go at this thing of life alone.

Sometimes people act like they can do it all on their own. They don't need help. They don't need friends. They hate group work. They won't play team sports. They think people will keep them from getting all the stuff done on their to-do lists.

Are they right? Um...definitely no!

Actually, I learned this lesson the hard way. After my friends rejected me in high school, I began to think things like, "This is no big deal; I can live my life on my own anyway." I told myself I didn't need anyone, and I could get through it. I focused in on myself and shut everyone else out.

I refused to reach out to others at school. Maybe I made a small effort here or there, but since no one just welcomed me with open arms, I quickly gave up. Looking back, I realize it would have been helpful for me to confide in my parents or coaches. Sure, it was easier to keep it bottled up the way I did, but it wasn't better. Opening up to someone would have given me perspective and helped me to move on more quickly. And thankfully, someone did eventually reach out to me. But, you'll hear more about that in the next chapter.

For now, just remember: No one can live life alone.

Think about football for a second. No one person can win a football game on his own. A quarterback with no linemen gets sacked every time. A single defensive lineman cannot stop the entire opposing line. Well, maybe I could have. Just kidding. It just won't work.

Or consider this story I heard: In Canada, an ox pull was being held to determine who had the strongest ox. The winner pulled 9,000 pounds, and the runner-up pulled just a few pounds short of that. A debate started about how much the two strongest oxen could pull if they were teamed together. People placed their bets. 16,000 pounds? 17,000 pounds? Maybe even double their singular efforts —18,000? When the two oxen were hitched together, they actually pulled over 26,000 pounds![1]

So what am I saying? I'm saying that you and your friends are like oxen...kind of.

I'm saying that a team can do more together than its members can do apart. You need a friend, even just one, who wants to see you reach your commitment as much as you do.

Seriously...with the support of a friend like that, you won't *just* succeed, you will be able to do more than you had even dreamed was possible.

THEY HELP US WHEN WE STRUGGLE.

Look, you just finished the chapter on Fighting for your commitment. You are going to have rough days. You're going to struggle to reach your goals. Sometimes, you'll need someone to have your back.

During the San Diego State game, I didn't know that I got called in because Simon Frasier had injured his ankle and needed to come out to get checked out by the medical team. That was what happened. But I didn't find out until later. I just knew I was needed. So I went in.

> A team can do more together than its members can do apart.

That is how OSU football worked. If someone went down, a teammate stepped in. There wasn't a long "Oh, no! What are we going to do?" discussion. We already knew. When Simon was hurt, I took his place, and the game went on.

One of these days, you're going to get hurt, too. And when that day comes, you'll need friends, good friends, who will stand with you and help you get through.

'Cause that's what friends do. Actually, it's what geese do, too.

"Geese, Joel? Seriously?"

Yes, Geese. You know...those annoying, big birds that take forever to cross the road, and when you honk at them they don't speed up, they just honk back...geese.

As dumb as they are when they cross the road, they actually do some cool stuff when they fly. Like, when they fly in V-formation, they work as a team. They actually take turns being the leader so the one at the center doesn't get too tired. When they aren't leading, they honk to encourage the leader to keep going. And when one gets hurt, two others land with it to help and protect it. They stick together until all three can fly again.[2]

That's support. That's teamwork. And that's what I'm talking about here. Surround yourself with good friends. Because they'll help you out on those really bad days when you need it most.

FINDING GOOD FRIENDS

Okay, so your friends are seriously important. Like milk in your cereal. Because, really, who likes dry cereal?

But let's be honest. You aren't going to ditch all your current friends in order to somehow find this "perfect" group of friends who will support you on your way to your commitments. Yeah, I agree...that just sounds stupid. And unrealistic.

So what am I talking about?

I'm talking about having a friend (or more than one) who IS the kind of person who will help you reach your goal. You don't have to have *only* these friends. But these kinds of friends are going to be necessary for you to reach your goal.

Look at what happened to me in high school. I thought I had a good team of friends who were all focused on the same goal. I was wrong. And I struggled because I had no one who was on my side.

Then I got to Ohio State. It was totally the opposite there. We were a good team. We all had the same goal: winning football games. But that didn't make *becoming* a team easy. Not by a long shot.

We all came from different backgrounds, communities, and cultures. We had guys in all different majors. We liked different types of music and movies and television shows. We had morning people and night owls. Some had girlfriends; others spent all their extra time in the weight room. We were over a hundred guys whose only real connection was that we were all members of the same football team, working together to win a national championship.

But we did it. We became a real team. And whether you have one friend or lots of friends who have your back, you will have to work at this kind of friendship, too.

So what does it take?

BE REAL.

Most of us have a lot of friends that we talk to every day or week. We say quick hellos in the hallway. We text about our plans for the weekend. We discuss the latest gossip, the scores from last night's basketball games, or how much we're looking forward to tonight's episode of *Glee*.

But we probably only have a couple of friends that we *really* talk to. There are probably only a couple of people out there who know the real you. Who know that you floss every night. Or that you are still afraid of clowns. Or that you never really got over your last boyfriend.

Am I right?

But when you make a big commitment, the kind we've been talking about here, you need to have people around who know the real you. These people are the ones who can keep you focused when you're facing a new challenge. These are the friends you turn to when you are discouraged and ready to give up. These are the ones who can make the difference between your failure and your success.

But letting people see the real you can be really hard.

I learned this lesson the hard way. Remember how my friends started partying and drinking? Well, I took the easy way out. I wasn't real with them. I was a really bad friend.

"Wait...you were the bad friend, Joel? They were the ones who ditched you."

Yeah, that's true. But I didn't do my part either. See, when we first started hanging out, we never actually *said* we'd do one thing or another. We made comments about the other 'losers' who were into drinking and partying. And we had a mutual understanding of each others' goals to be good athletes.

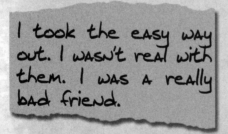

But it was all unspoken. So when push came to shove, it was just easier to overlook this 'mutual understanding' because we'd never said it out loud. When Brandon first went out drinking with another group, we were all so shocked that we didn't know what to say to him.

So we did the worst thing possible: we said nothing. We let it slide. We avoided the conflict.

We knew he was off track. We knew he was out of line. What he was doing was the opposite of what our group stood for. But we kept our mouths shut.

Why? Because it was easier. And sadly, I just kept making that same mistake.

As more of my friends started partying, I never spoke up. I was hoping that my refusal to participate might bring them back in line. But it didn't work...surprise, surprise. Because I kept quiet, my friends could think whatever they wanted about my choice to not drink. Some of my friends thought, "Joel is not drinking with us, he must think he is better than us." Of course that wasn't true. But I never set the record straight. I never sat down and had it out with them. I avoided the conflict entirely.

I wasn't real with them, and it cost me all of my friends.

Don't make the same mistake I did in this area. Trust your friends enough to let them see the real you. Don't pretend all is well when it isn't. Be willing to be a little vulnerable.

Say out loud what you're really thinking. You have to admit your mistakes and where you're struggling. Otherwise, how will they know? Speak up and tell them what's really going on. Your friends will be able to help you keep moving forward in areas that might have kept you from standing firm in your commitment.

Don't be afraid to be real with your friends. They probably already know enough dirt on you to keep you from running for president. So being real with them about your commitment probably won't be too much worse. And having them around can make all the difference.

BE REALISTIC

If you want the kind of friends who can help you toward your goals, you have to be real with them. That's just how it works.

Sorry.

But you also have to be realistic about your friends. Not every friend you have will be the kind of person you should be that open with. Admit it, some of your friends can't keep secrets. What they know...everyone knows. So sharing your commitments with them may not be wise.

Do you have to stop being friends with them? Of course not!

I'm not saying you have to choose people based *entirely* on their ability to keep a secret. I'm just saying...be careful which friends you share your commitment with.

Pick the friends who build you up. Who value commitments. Who have goals in their own lives. Pick the friends who will keep you moving forward.

It's a super old saying, but it's still true: "We become like the people we hang out with." I *thought* I had found a group of guys who had the same commitment I did, but really, it wasn't true. I had decided not to drink or party. I *thought* my friends agreed. But we turned out to have totally different ideas about the party scene. And in the end, I had to choose between them and my commitment. Because the truth is, if I had stayed with my friends in high school, I can almost guarantee that I would've started drinking, too.

Don't make my mistake. I was not realistic about my friends and where they stood. And when they dumped me, I had no one else to depend on. Look at your friends and pick one or two who will support you and hold you accountable.

Choose the best ones, and you will have a huge advantage in reaching your goal.

BE RIGHT THERE

One of the best things that we did at Ohio State to become a good team was to be together.

Everything we did prepared us to play as one. We practiced together, wore the same gear, followed the same rules. We even took a test at the end of preseason camp on our teammates' names and hometowns. We spent time getting to know each other so that we could be the "family" we wanted to be.

And we had a lot of traditions that helped us feel united.

The best example of this is our pregame routine. For 24 hours before every home game, we did the same things in the same order. Preparing for the game together helped us play together when we took the field. It forced us to put the rest of our lives away for those moments to focus on a common goal: winning a football game.

Let me walk you through the weekly ritual.

24 hours to kickoff: The Team Arrives
On Friday night, we met at The Woody and took buses to the Ohio State golf course. We gathered at our practice facility in team-issued warm-ups for a light practice and meetings. From this moment on, we had no more interaction with the outside world.

19 hours to kickoff: The Team Dinner
The OSU golf course hosted our exquisite pregame dinner. We entered together and stood behind our chairs until one of the team captains said a quick prayer. The seniors always went through the buffet line first, and the rest of us sat with our position group to wait our turn. My group was the D-Line. The food was incredible. Most guys got two plates and dipped much of their meal in ranch dressing. Then, as if the meal didn't already include everything we could want, servers regularly came to the table to ask if we needed anything. Since I love chocolate milk, I would politely request a glass. And by the time I was a senior, my chocolate milk was sitting on the table waiting for me before we entered the room. Awesome! After we'd eaten all we could stand (which was a lot), we left for the hotel.

15 hours to kickoff: Team chapel.

At the hotel, we had team chapel, where a former player or community leader shared an inspirational message, and then we watched a highlight film. We finished the meeting by singing *Carmen Ohio,* OSU's alma mater, on one knee and in the softest whisper. After the meeting we received our nighttime snack, which included two amazing rice crispy treats. By the time I was a senior, my teammates knew that I was madly in love with the rice crispy treats, and I got at least a dozen each week.

4.5 hours to kickoff: Team Walk

In the morning we woke up and put on our team sweats for the traditional 'team walk.' It took less than five minutes to walk around a small building. But it was part of the tradition. And we never missed the Walk.

4 hours to kickoff: Pregame meal

We ate our pregame meal exactly 4 hours before kickoff. And during this time, that week's honorary captain addressed the team.

2 hours to kickoff: The Walk to the Stadium

Nearly two hours before kickoff, we walked together, dressed in suits and ties, to St. John Arena, where thousands of fans gathered for a pregame band concert. Fans screamed for autographs and pictures as we walked through and waited as Coach Tressel spoke to the crowd. Then we continued on to our stadium, "The Horseshoe," and made our way to our locker room. We prepared for the game and anxiously awaited our turn for warm-ups.

45 minutes to kickoff: Team Hive

When the final group arrived on the field for warm-ups, we had our 'team hive.' We linked arms and slowly walked from the far Southeast corner of the end zone to the middle of the end zone. When we approached the middle of the end zone, the hive would swing and make a 90 degree turn to the right. The cheers of the crowd escalated at this point and always tempted us to break the hive early, but we would stay together as a team until the turn was complete. Finally, with the length of the field in front of us, we charged ahead and met together in the center of the field, pumping each other up for the game ahead. We excitedly returned to our locker room and awaited Coach Tressel.

10 minutes to kickoff: Team Prayer

With only a few minutes until kickoff, Coach Tressel called us together in the locker room. Coach would take a knee and we silently followed his lead. We held hands and prayed together, and then in unison recited a poem that always gave me perspective. *"I am only one. But I am one. I can't do everything, but I can do something, and that I can do I ought to do, and what I ought to do by the grace of God I shall do."*

Kickoff: Play as a team...play as a family

I was only one, but we were a team. I could not beat the opponent, but we could. Our traditions brought us together, but it was up to us to stay together.

We were a team.

Of course, that is what the Ohio State Buckeyes do before a home game. And of course, I'm not suggesting that your friends have to have a team hive or eat rice crispy treats together.

"I AM only oNe. But I AM oNe. I cAN't do everything, but I cAN do something."

What I am saying is that a good team is united. Every group of friends has a common bond. Sometimes it's not a good thing (like drinking or drugs). But mostly it's that they share a common interest. Or they share a common desire to reach a goal. And by being together, they motivate each other towards that goal.

That's what I'm talking about. You have to be real. You have to be realistic.

But most of all, you have to be right there. Because we were together, as a team, we could help each other. We could depend on each other. And we could play (and win) football games together.

The same is true for you. When you find those few people who will support, encourage, and help you, standing your ground becomes much easier, and the final rewards will be far beyond what you imagined they could be.

You might even win a National Championship.

MAKING IT PERSONAL

1. This chapter focused on the value of having the right friends. Think about your friends. Which ones can you count on to support your commitment? Make a list.

_____

_____

_____

2. Joel says that friends can help us when we struggle. Have you ever experienced this? How have your friends helped you in tough times? Or have you ever helped someone else?

_____

_____

_____

3. Do you think that 'being real' with your friends is truly important? Why or why not? Do you find it hard to 'be real' with your friends? Do you think they can 'be real' with you?

_____

_____

_____

4. Sometimes 'being real' means telling a friend that you disagree with what he or she is doing. Joel shared how he regrets not doing this with his friends. Can you see yourself confronting your friends when you know they are doing something wrong? Why or why not?

_____

_____

_____

5. Think about the concept of 'being right there' for your friends. Joel talked about how every Buckeye player knew that his teammates had his back. Do your friends know that you support them in their good decisions? If not, how could you let them know?

_____

_____

_____

6. What kinds of things do you think you and your friends could accomplish if you intentionally work together as a team to help each other keep your commitments?

_____

_____

_____

CHAPTER 8:

FAILURE?

"What happened to Ben"

Ben was the class clown. He was hilarious. He was also one of my closest friends.

Ben was funny, and he knew it. As a kid, he'd act up just to get attention. In school, he could keep an entire class laughing if the teacher let him.

Even at home, Ben was the kind of guy people wanted to be around. At Christmas, his family would beg him to do impressions for them. He could imitate Mick Jagger, Robert De Niro,

> In school, he could keep an entire class laughing if the teacher let him.

and all of his family members. He was so good, he could make his grandmother pee her pants. Every year. And then, as she cleaned up her accident, Ben made it his goal to make her go again, just to make everyone else laugh harder.

Ben had a gift. And he had a dream. He wanted to be an entertainer. In high school, Ben made the school musical his freshman year. He only got a small role, but he was really good. And it confirmed his passion. He was going to make it as an entertainer. He committed himself to pursuing that goal.

For most of high school, Ben fit perfectly into our group. He wasn't an athlete, but he was focused. He was silly, but he was also motivated. He knew what he wanted to do with his life, and he was driven to succeed.

Until our junior year.

That was the year that my friends slid into the party scene. And Ben went along. He wasn't one of the first, but eventually, he joined in. He knew that partying wouldn't help him to succeed, but at the time, he just didn't think about it. Fitting in was more important. His friends were all he had. So he let others make the decision for him.

See, Ben never knew his dad. And in high school, his mom lost custody of him, so he moved in with his grandmother. He was lonely and hurt. And the drinking and partying made him feel better...for a while. Then he met Josh. Josh had his own group of friends, and Ben started to hang out with them, doing whatever they were doing. And what they were doing was drugs. Before long, Ben was getting high almost every day of the week. He was addicted.

But Ben's grandmother wasn't stupid. She knew what he was doing and that he was constantly lying to her. So, she threw him out. One night Ben came home to find a pile of trash bags on the front lawn. And he couldn't get in the house. His key didn't work; the locks had been changed. He went back to the front yard to look at the bags again.

The bags were filled with his clothes and possessions. And on one of the bags, Ben found a note: "Ben, if this is what you are going to be doing with your life then you aren't going to be staying here." He was shocked. He knew his grandmother wasn't happy with him, but didn't think of her as the confrontational type. And to change the locks? Wow, she must have been serious.

With no place to go, he called Josh. He spent the night on Josh's couch, thinking. His dad, his mom, his grandmother. They had all abandoned him. All of a sudden Josh, a guy whom nobody took seriously, was the only person in his life. Ben had never felt so alone.

But there was still one person he trusted: Mr. Giffin, the Chemistry teacher. Ben and I were both in his class, and he was a great teacher. He was in his forties, but he related well to his students. You could tell that he really cared about you as a person. He especially cared about Ben. Where other teachers didn't get along with Ben, Mr. Giffin got him. He knew how to handle him in class without discouraging or disrespecting him. They had a great relationship.

But one Thursday night, Mr. Giffin went for a jog and didn't come home. He died, very unexpectedly, in the middle of his run. His death was a huge shock for the town and the school. But it hit Ben even harder. The announcement was made in our school auditorium. Ben broke down and sobbed for hours. His grandmother had kicked him out, and now the only other adult who respected him had died. Could his life get any worse?

He decided he didn't want to find out.

That day, Ben started to make some changes in his life. He called his grandmother and asked to come home. She agreed, as long as he gave up drinking and drugs. So he did. It was a turning point for Ben. He had lost sight of his commitment and his dream. He had let other people lead him instead of choosing for himself. Now he was ready to start over. He renewed his commitment, and he began again.

And it was hard. Really hard. Not only did he have to deal with his addictions, he had to deal with his old friends who didn't get why he'd quit. They didn't believe him. They certainly didn't encourage him. They mostly made fun of him.

He had let other people lead him instead of choosing for himself. Now he was ready to start over.

Again Ben found himself depressed and alone. This time, however, he let himself experience the pain, and that helped him to heal. He talked a lot about life with his grandmother. He thought about his choices and where they had taken him. He decided, for the first time, to be responsible for his own decisions instead of blaming his problems on other people.

It was tough. But he realized he was strong. That he could do really hard things on his own. And...that he was not alone. He realized he knew someone else in the same boat as he was. He called me.

Ben reached out to me and apologized for how he had acted towards me when our group started to drink. I was grateful for his gesture. We hung out a lot after that. Ben was happy to have a friendship that didn't depend on drugs and alcohol. I was happy to be there for a friend.

But, even clean and refocused on his commitment, nothing went easy for Ben. He still didn't quite know how to make his dream of being an entertainer a reality. And show business is a hard field to break into. He had no plan, so he made himself an opportunity.

He moved to Chicago. He had $300, no job, and no place to stay. But he went. A friend offered him a place to stay. He worked minimum wage jobs. He finally got a job as an assistant manager at a pizza place. But it didn't last long. A lot of the guys hired there were fresh from prison, and some were still into drugs and crime. Ben knew he couldn't be around that stuff, even if the job did pay his rent.

So he quit. He still hadn't gotten a break, but he kept on trying. Finally, a friend let him move in rent-free, and he could focus on his career. He went to auditions and sent out resumes and head shots. Still nothing. He was really tempted to go back to drugs, but again, he stood his ground.

Then, one day, he tried a new strategy. Stand-up comedy. After all, he'd been a comedian all his life. And with all the 'open mic' nights at local comedy clubs, it might just be the break he'd been looking for.

So he did it. One night, Ben walked over to a club called 'Frankie J's' and signed his name on the open mic list. The club was dark and dingy. There were dusty, old theatre seats occupying the space. But the crowd seemed to be about his age, so that was promising.

Before long, it was his turn to go on stage. When his name was called, he began to panic. "I have absolutely no idea of what to do to entertain these people!" he thought. He slowly moved to the stage, doubting his decision the entire way.

But when he grabbed the mic and faced the crowd, the fears and doubts disappeared. He knew exactly what to do. He began doing impressions of famous people, just like he had done for his family at Christmas. To his surprise and relief, the crowd laughed! It was his first real break.

Things slowly began to move forward for Ben. He kept working the local clubs, getting experience and honing his skills. And it worked for him. Ben now owns and operates the most successful comedy club in downtown Chicago. He's also become a film producer. He manages other comedians' careers and has started his own non-profit company that supports creative arts programs in public schools.

And it all started because he failed.

FAILURE HAPPENS

"But Joel," you're probably thinking, "I try to avoid failure. I hate to fail."

Well, I hate it, too. And I don't think anyone should purposely throw a game or fail a test or mess up a friendship. But let's be honest. We can't avoid failure. It is part of every person's life. Big or small, failure is going to happen.

"But, Joel, haven't you already talked about this...you know, how life sucks?"

Yep, we did cover that. But this is different. See, "be ready when bad stuff happens" really means sometimes other people or circumstances are going to mess things up for you. That is not what I'm talking about here.

This is about when YOU mess things up.

This is about you not studying and flunking the test. This is when you forget the words to your solo in the Spring Choir concert... in front of the whole school. This is you forgetting to call your parents and tell them you'll be late. It's when you pick up too many books at once and drop them all over the floor.

You can blame other people if you want. But when it comes right down to it...you screwed up.

And even though lots of people try to pretend that they don't mess up, it's just not true. You aren't always going to say the right thing, do the right thing, choose the right option. You're going to fail.

And when you make a commitment, it's even

> You aren't always going to say the right thing, do the right thing, choose the right option.

more guaranteed. The fact is, when you set a real commitment for yourself, something big and significant...you're going to have to deal with failure. You are going to try something that you think will get you closer to your goal, and it won't work.

Like Ben. He decided that moving to Chicago would get him closer to his goal. It was a risk, he knew. But he decided he needed to go where the entertainment jobs were. Did it work? Eventually.

But for years, literally years, he failed. He had no good job and no place to live. He went on lots of auditions, but he didn't get a single role. Even after he tried stand-up, he failed. Not every joke he told was a hit. Not every impression got a laugh.

What's my point? Failure happens. You're going to screw up. And you need to be able to deal with that fact.

FEARLESS

So how do you deal with it? Failure, I mean.

Well, first of all, don't let failure stop you before you start.

A lot of people do that. For them, the possibility of failure is so frightening that they just freeze. They do nothing. Oh, they want to succeed. They really do. But they are afraid that, if they try to do something significant, they might fail. They want to avoid falling on their faces more than they want to succeed.

So they just don't start. And honestly, this happens to a lot of us.

We might be cut. So we don't try out.
She might say 'no.' So we don't ask her out.

They want to avoid falling on their faces more than they want to succeed.

145

You might not get the job. So you just don't apply.

And where do we end up? Locked in our rooms, taking no risks as all. Not a fun way to live, right?

So what about you?

Maybe what I'm describing here is just where you are. Maybe you've been wanting to make a commitment, a really big one, but the idea that you might not reach it is holding you back. Maybe you're thinking, "Sure, Joel, I have a dream, but I'll never get there. So why even try?"

Why? Because *purposely short-changing yourself and your commitments because of your fears is not a path to significance.* Setting low expectations may keep you from ever having to deal with something going wrong, but it also won't move you forward.

The fact is, if the fear of failure is your only reason not to try, you've already failed.

So just get over it. Don't let the fear of "what might happen" stand in your way.

Will there be consequences if you fail? Probably. You might get laughed at. You might have to start over or do it again, repeat a class, pay more money, apologize to someone. But who cares? Nobody is perfect. Nobody expects you to be perfect. But you'll always regret it if you don't even try.

OPPORTUNITY KNOCKS

Besides, failure doesn't mean you'll never achieve your goal. Look at Ben. Ben succeeded because he failed. If he hadn't failed, he wouldn't have succeeded. Simple as that.

"Um, Joel, are we still talking about the same thing here? I mean, doesn't failure sort of mean...that you failed? Isn't that the end?"

Well, yes...and no.

Just think about it. Instead of being something to dread, failure can actually open up a world of opportunity. It actually opens the door to amazing new possibilities.

Consider this. Failure *can* mean that you should stop doing something. You ask the girl out. She refuses you while laughing hysterically at the thought of going out with you. You failed to get the date. And based on her reaction, you should probably let her go.

But sometimes, failure just means that one attempt didn't work. And you still have others you could try.

You ask the girl out. She says no. But she quickly adds that it's because she already has plans. You failed to get the date, right? Yep. Is it the end? Maybe not. The door of opportunity is still open. You could still get a date with her for next weekend.

That's what I'm talking about here. You have to start seeing failure as a beginning, not an end. It's not getting a final answer, it's getting the chance to ask a new question. It's a new opportunity to rethink, revise and start again.

> You have to start seeing failure as a beginning, not an end.

And it's absolutely necessary. We need to fail.

"What?!? Joel, have you lost it?"

No, really. Just think about it. We need to fail to learn new things. In fact, we wouldn't learn anything if it weren't for failure. Sure, "trial-and-error" sounds better. But what we really mean is we learn from our mistakes.

We don't learn to ride a bike without falling down.

We don't figure out how to tie our shoes perfectly the first time.

We lose a lot of lives in a new video game before we get to the highest levels.

Getting good at something just doesn't "happen." It takes commitment to improve at something that is new or something that is difficult. It takes hard work. And it takes failure. Because failure is an opportunity to learn things that you wouldn't have learned otherwise.

Do you know the TV show, *MythBusters*? Okay, I realize it's a "science" show. But seriously, they live by this idea. Their motto is "Failure is always an option!" Every time they run an experiment, they get more information. Even if they don't get the result they were hoping for, they still learned something that will help them make the experiment better the next time.

Now don't get me wrong...failure sucks. It hurts. But it can also be the best way to learn about life, yourself, and how to keep your commitments.

That's what happened for both Ben and me. If I hadn't failed at basketball and baseball, I might never have discovered how much I loved football. If Ben hadn't struggled like he did, he would never have learned how to keep going during tough times.

So failure is an opportunity to learn new things. But it's also a chance to try a different approach.

I mean, let's be honest. We usually like to have this perfect plan for how we're going to accomplish something. At least, in our heads, it seems perfect. We know just where we're going. We'll achieve our dreams in no time.

And then, failure strikes. You run out of money. You make a big mistake. You and your best friend stop speaking. And your plan falls apart...just like that.

So do you give up in disgust? Just quit pursuing your commitment because your plan didn't work?

Of course not!

Because when you fail, you are forced to try something new. You have to change from Plan A to Plan B. You have to think outside the box. You have to take a chance.

Think of Ben. He failed, lots of times, in Chicago. He auditioned for lots of jobs and got none. So he tried something new - stand-up. And it worked. But it was his failures that forced him to think outside his box.

> You have to think outside the box. You have to take a chance.

Or think of my sister, Sara. She had a commitment to get a great education. Her plan was to go to an Ivy League school. But money was a problem. So she had to consider other possibilities. And that's how she learned about the Naval Academy. It wasn't her original plan. It was definitely outside her comfort zone. But it was exactly the path she needed to take. And it lead to her reaching her goal.

It works the same for you. Failure doesn't have to bring your commitment to a screeching halt. It can give you the chance to learn something new. Or to try a path you might never have tried before. And it might be just that knowledge or that path that opens the door to the success you are dreaming of.

GET OVER IT

So what do you do? When you really mess things up, what do you do?

Well, I can tell you what NOT to do. Don't overreact.

Typically, that's our first instinct, isn't it? We freak out and jump three steps ahead and say, "Crap, I missed the due date on my homework, now I'm going to get a bad grade, and it's going to bring down my GPA, and I'll never get into college."

You missed one assignment...it's not the end of the world! Okay, you screwed up. But don't beat yourself up. Just make the best of that situation. Make it a learning experience. And then move forward again.

And when you do screw up on the path to your commitment, what is the next step?

You do exactly the same thing. You get over it! You change your attitude so that you can move past your failures. You might be embarrassed. Or discouraged. You might want to quit. That's normal. But at some point, you move on. At some point, you let go of the self-pity and decide to keep going.

I had to do that. More than once. And if I had let failures discourage me from moving forward, I would never have achieved my goals. I would never have played for the Buckeyes. Or started speaking. Or written a book.

> At some point, you let go of the self-pity and decide to keep going.

Ben had to do it, too. And through his failures, he learned a lot of stuff that helped him succeed.

- He learned the importance of commitment and accountability.
- He learned how to resist temptation.
- He learned responsibility and how to think and make decisions for himself.
- He gained the confidence that was absolutely crucial to surviving his first years in Chicago.
- He made important business connections and learned how the film and comedy industry works.

So what about you? Are you still letting failure keep you from your commitments?

Ben and I chose to move past our mistakes. You can choose to keep going forward, too. To pursue a life of significance does mean that we have to risk failures. Failure will most likely happen, BUT failure may provide us exactly the opportunities we need to keep our goals. Even if you fail, keep moving forward.

It was worth it for me. And for Ben. And it will be worth it for you when you succeed, too.

MAKING IT PERSONAL

1. We all know that failure happens. Sometimes it's funny like when you drop your books in the hallway. Can you think of a time that you or someone you know failed in a funny way? Write it down here.

   _____

   _____

   _____

2. Can you think of another example where you or someone you know experienced failure that wasn't funny? Was it the end of the world? What happened after that?

   _____

   _____

   _____

3. Everyone fears failure, at least to some extent. Joel says that using fear as an excuse not to even try is the easy way out. What problems might come from letting 'fear of failure' control your life?

   _____

   _____

   _____

4. Do you agree that failure can be seen as an opportunity, not an end? Why or why not?

   _____

   _____

   _____

5.   Think about a time you, or someone you know, failed.
      What did you (or they) learn from that experience? Were
      you (or they) able to do something that was positive as a
      result of that mistake?

      _____

      _____

      _____

6.   Sometimes failure gets the best of people because they
      aren't able or willing to try new things. Are you some-
      one who's willing to 'think outside the box,' or do you
      like to follow a plan? How can you prepare yourself to
      try new things as you pursue your new commitment?

      _____

      _____

      _____

CONCLUSION

I stood on the field that night in total disbelief.

The game was over. The season was over.

And The Ohio State Buckeyes had clinched the National Championship!

Fireworks, confetti, and complete chaos surrounded me on all sides. Swarms of Buckeye fans and media flooded the field. I watched the awards ceremony in amazement. It was a moment I will never forget as long as I live.

But that amazing experience would not have been possible except for a very different moment. When a twelve-year old kid got out of bed, all alone, and did push-ups until he was exhausted. There was no confetti. No TV cameras. No trophy. No commemorative ring.

It was just me, making a decision that would affect the rest of my life. I made a huge commitment to be the best football player I could be. And I never looked back.

Was it easy? Of course not.

Was it a lot of work? Yep.

Were there days I wanted to forget it and give up? For sure. Lots of them.

But I knew what I wanted. I wanted to live a life of Significance. I wanted my life to matter, in a big way. So I committed myself to football. I worked until I was physically strong. I practiced until I was totally prepared for every play. On and off the field,

I focused on my goal, taking one step at a time until I had done what I set out to do.

And what did it take? It took a lot of Faith in myself and my dream. And my Faith kept me going on the toughest days. It wasn't easy; I had to Fight for every step forward. It cost me some friendships, but I also found some Friends who supported me all the way to my goal. And it took Failure. There were lots of lessons learned the hard way, many of which I have already shared with you.

But I did it. I stood my ground.

And as I stood on the field that night, basking in the glory of a National Championship with my teammates, I realized that keeping my commitments, no matter what, was really what made all the difference.

It's such a simple thing, really. But in the end, it set me apart. It made me part of something so much bigger than that junior high kid could have guessed was possible. And I can tell you this. It was worth it.

It was all worth it.

So that's my challenge to you: Make your commitment. Pursue it with all your heart. *Stand your Ground*. And you, too, will find yourself achieving things you never dreamed were possible.

> It's such a simple thing, really. But in the end, it set me apart.

ENDNOTES

[1] Angier, Michael. "Synergy - One Plus One Equals Three?" *Expert Marketing Support*. Web. 15 Sept. 2010. <http://www.smithfam.com/news2/synergy.html>.

[2] Swindoll, Chuck. "Geese." Letter. Oct. 1991. *Crosswalk.com*. Web. 15 Sept. 2010. <http://www.crosswalk.com/pastors/illustrations/>.

ACKNOWLEDGEMENTS

This book was truly a team effort. It could not have been done without the valuable contributions of my good friends Ryan and Emily Holliday, Ken Gordon, Chris Lundquist and Shannah Hogue. You guys rock!

My football and wrestling coaches have been some of the most influential people in my life. Thank you to all the men who took the time and patience to coach me over the years. And a special thank you to Coach Temple, Coach Ramsay, Coach Hood, Coach Heacock and Coach Tressel.

I have the best parents in the world. Thank you, Mom and Dad. Your love and support has made me the man that I am today. I thank God for you.

Bethany, you're still smoking hot!

Joel III and Judah, here we go!